SYNTHETIC ECONOMICS

Also published in

Reprints Of Economic Classics

By Henry Ludwell Moore

Economic Cycles Their Law & Cause [1914]

Forecasting The Yield & The Price Of Cotton [1917]

Generating Economic Cycles [1923]

Laws Of Wages [1911]

SYNTHETIC ECONOMICS

BY

HENRY LUDWELL MOORE

PROFESSOR OF POLITICAL ECONOMY IN COLUMBIA UNIVERSITY

"L'unification synthétique qui transforme une
pluralité discontinue de faits en un réseau continu
de relations."

LÉON BRUNSCHVICG

REPRINTS OF ECONOMIC CLASSICS

AUGUSTUS M. KELLEY · PUBLISHERS
NEW YORK · 1967

First Edition 1929

(New York: The Macmillan Company, 1929)

Reprinted 1967 by

AUGUSTUS M. KELLEY PUBLISHERS

Library of Congress Catalogue Card Number
67-18571

CONTENTS

CHAPTER I

INTRODUCTION

CHAPTER II

FUNDAMENTAL NOTIONS

CHAPTER III

THE LAW OF DEMAND

CHAPTER IV

THE LAW OF SUPPLY

CHAPTER V

MOVING EQUILIBRIA

CHAPTER VI

ECONOMIC OSCILLATIONS

CHAPTER VII

CONCLUSION

SYNTHETIC ECONOMICS

SYNTHETIC ECONOMICS

CHAPTER I

INTRODUCTION

The mathematical approach to economic theory bifurcated at an early point in its course. One road, travelled chiefly by practical men intent upon the exigent business of the day, has led through a dreary region directly to practical, but unrelated, results; the other road, followed mainly by philosophers with primary interest in causes and relations, has ascended to picturesque heights affording distant views of the ensemble of economic activity, but has stopped short amid the enchanting scene and left the explorers in doubt as to what might be the real destination of so promising a beginning.

Two Approaches to Economic Theory

In 1874 when Léon Walras had just published the early instalment of his demonstration of the theory of general equilibrium, he wrote a letter to the aged Cournot which contains a sentence marking the divergence of the two roads to economic theory:

"Notre méthode est la même, car la mienne est la vôtre, seulement vous vous placez immédiatement au bénéfice de *la loi des grands nombres* et sur le chemin qui mène aux applications numériques. Et moi, je demeure en deçà de cette loi sur le terrain des données rigoureuses et de la pure théorie."

1

Both Cournot and Walras employed the mathematical method, but Cournot entered upon a course which seemed adapted to lead, through the use of the theory of probabilities, to numerical applications; while Walras concentrated his strength upon the solution of a central problem in pure theory and made no effort whatever to obtain an empirical test of the adequacy of his theoretical construction in the interpretation of the world of economic realities.

The central problem to the solution of which Walras gave his life was the interdependence of all economic quantities and the necessity of expressing in simultaneous mathematical equations the conditions of their common determination. To facilitate his inquiry he created an hypothetical static state having the properties that are familiar to all students of economic theory. His solution of the problem of the mathematical conditions of equilibrium in a static state inspired an ideal conception of the goal toward which future investigators must work: A comprehensive treatment of economic questions in a changing society must take cognizance of the interdependence of all types of economic change, and the only kind of treatment that will lead to rational forecasting and control is mathematical in character.

Cournot had a clear conception of the interdependence of the parts of the economic system and he stated very compactly the difficulties with which the economist is confronted:

"So far we have studied how, for each commodity by itself, the law of demand, in connection with the conditions of production of that commodity, determines the price of it and regulates the incomes of its producers. We considered as given and invariable the prices of other commodities and the incomes of other producers; but in reality the economic system is a whole of which all the parts are connected and react on each other. An increase in the income of the producers of commodity A will affect the demand for the commodities B, C, etc., and the incomes of their producers, and, by its reactions, will involve a change in the demand for commodity A. It seems, therefore, as if, for a complete and rigorous solution of the problems relative to some parts of the economic system, it were indispensable to take the entire system into consideration. But this would surpass the powers of mathematical analysis and of our practical methods of calculation, even if the values of all the constants could be assigned to them numerically." [1] He abandoned the forbidding task of determining concretely the conditions of a general equilibrium and sought, by other means, to reach approximate solutions of special problems affecting the general economic system.

Cournot's results were published in 1838; Walras', in 1874–77. Cournot's mastery of the theory of probability was, in his day, so great that Poisson conceded his priority in the conception and development of ideas that subsequently appeared in the latter's *Probabilités des jugements;* while Czuber, a careful historian of the theory of probability, has ranked him second only to Laplace in his grasp of the philosophy of chance. But in the half century since Cournot's

---

[1] Cournot: *Researches into the Mathematical Principles of the Theory of Wealth.* Bacon's translation, p. 127.

death the development of the theory of probability has entered upon an entirely new phase, and the supplying of statistical material affording the means of immediate application in economic questions has become the special function of bureaus, public and private, in many parts of the world. Walras' successors, while extending his work, have for the most part followed his example of remaining in the domain of pure theory, and in certain cases have even deprecated any attempt to pass to a statistical investigation of the questions to which they have devoted such eminent ability. Notwithstanding this attitude of the *École de Lausanne*, the idea that economic theory may be fruitfully approached through the conception of the equilibrium of the interdependent parts has made such headway since the publication of Walras' epochal essays that Pantaleoni, with perhaps pardonable exaggeration, could say, in 1909, "*l'economia si presenta ora quale scienza delle leggi dell'equilibrio economico.*"

The thought that inevitably presents itself to an investigator in touch with these collateral developments is whether, equipped with the new tools and supplied with the new material, he may not advisedly reconsider the problem abandoned by Cournot in 1838 and left as a pure statical theory by Walras in 1877. Is it not possible to solve the problem dynamically and to give, by means of recent statistical methods, a concrete, practical form to the theoretical ideas of moving equilibria, oscillations, and secular change?

The Scope of Synthetic Economics

The title of this essay, *Synthetic Economics*, is intended to indicate a concrete, positive description of moving equilibria, oscillations, and secular change, by a method which presents all of the interrelated economic quantities in a synthesis of simultaneous, real equations.

As far as I am aware neither Walras nor Pareto used the term *Synthetic Economics*. Pareto insists upon the need, in every science, of following up the work of analysis with synthesis; [2] he uses repeatedly the adjective *synthetic* to describe the peculiar point of view of Walras and himself in their use of mathematics in the treatment of economic theory; [3] but it seems that the definite collocation of the words *synthetic economics* did not appear in his work. Barone and Sensini use casually the exact expression *synthetic economics* in describing the method of Walras and Pareto as a presentation of the whole of statical economics in a series of simultaneous equations.[4]

Another Italian economist, quite unconnected with the School of Lausanne, Professor Loria, uses as the title of one of his works *La Sintesi Economica*, which

[2] Pareto: *Cours d'économie politique.* Vol. 1, p. 13.

[3] Pareto: "Nota sulle equazioni dell'equilibrio dinamico." *Giornale degli Economisti*, Settembre 1901, p. 14.

[4] "Cournot, Walras, Pareto, le cui opere contengono più che un'intera biblioteca, sono i grandi maestri della nuova economia *sintetica*." Enrico Barone: *Principi di Economia Politica*, 1908, p. 25 n.

"È questo uno dei principali vantaggi della moderna economia *sintetica*, che apparsa per la prima volta colle immortali ricerche di Walras. . . ." Guido Sensini: *La Teoria della Rendita*, 1912, pp. 157–158.

approaches in form, but not in substance, the title borne by the present essay.

There are three special characteristics which I should like the name *Synthetic Economics* to imply: (1) the use of simultaneous equations to express the *consensus* of exchange, production, capitalization, and distribution; (2) the extension of the use of this mathematical synthesis into economic dynamics where all of the variables in the constituent problems are treated as functions of time; and (3) the still further extension of the synthesis to the point of giving the equations concrete, statistical forms. With these implications *Synthetic Economics* is both deductive and inductive; dynamic, positive, and concrete.

A first advantage of this method of treating as an ensemble the totality of prices and their determinants is the elimination of many controversies in economics as to the causes of phenomena. Is the cause of the value of a commodity its cost of production or its marginal utility? Is the cause of the rate of interest the productivity of capital or the discount of future goods? Is the cause of the rate of wages the laborer's standard of living or the marginal value of his product? In the history of economic theory these questions have been discussed to the point, not of the conversion of the disputants, but of the exhaustion of their faculties. Yet when a synthetic view of exchange, production, capitalization, and distribution is taken, we see at once that each of the alternatives of the preceding questions contains a partial truth; that the sum of the partial truths is not the whole truth; that the proper weight and place of each partial truth may be specified; and that the ensemble of the determining conditions may be mathematically expressed.

A second advantage of the synthetic method is that it enables one to know when an economic problem has reached a solution. Here, a distinction should be made in the meaning of the word "solution" according as one sees it from the point of view of the mathematical, or of the synthetic method. The problem is solved by the mathematical method when there are as many independent equations as there are unknown quantities in the problem. From the point of view of the synthetic method, however, this is only half of the solution: over and above the presentation of the abstract simultaneous equations, proof must be supplied that the equations themselves may be empirically derived and, consequently, that the problem admits of a real solution. For example, we know that Marshall regarded Note xxi in the "Mathematical Appendix" of his *Principles* as embodying "a bird's-eye view of the problems of joint demand, composite demand, joint supply and composite supply when they all arise together." As a mathematical economist he seemed to be satisfied, for he says: "however complex the problem may become, we can see that it is theoretically determinate, because the number of unknowns is always exactly equal to the number of the equations which we obtain." Marshall devoted his genius throughout a long, laborious life to an endeavor to give a realistic form to the abstract equations of Note xxi. Did he, from the point of view of the synthetic method, reach his goal? Every demand equation and every supply equation that figures in Note xxi is a function simply of one variable. The work of Marshall affords no method of deriving concretely either a demand equation or a supply equation; it affords no cogent reason for believing that, if methods for deriving the equations were devised, either demand or supply could, as a function of one variable alone, be expressed with sufficient accuracy to be useful in the treatment of real problems. Note xxi may be a possible, abstract mathematical solution of the problem Marshall had in mind, but economists will differ as to whether it may suggest a useful first step towards a concrete, real solution, and no opinion can be more than a lucky guess until methods have been devised for submitting the mathematical formulation to an empirical test.

A third, and by far the chief, advantage of the synthetic method is that it gives ground for the hope of introducing into economic life rational forecasting and enlightened control.

The synthetic method is concerned with the ensemble of prices and their determinants. Suppose it is assumed,

   (i)   that the laws of supply and demand in a changing society may be empirically ascertained;

  (ii)   that all of the conditions determining a moving general equilibrium may be statistically expressed;

 (iii)   that it is possible to know concretely the results of the solution of the simultaneous equations expressing a moving general equilibrium.

Under these conditions, it is possible to obtain a rational forecast of the result of changing, in any definite way, any factor in the moving general equilibrium. But in social life, to foreknow the effect, qualitative and quantitative, of specific change is to possess, precisely, the *sine qua non* of enlightened control. The problem of the rational forecasting of oscillations about the moving equilibrium introduces a complexity similar to that of forecasting the demand for a single commodity from a knowledge of its demand function. A first approximation in the latter problem is reached by considering the demand for the commodity as a simple function of its price. A second approximation in the accuracy of the predicted demand is obtained by regarding the demand as a function of many prices. In case of oscillations about the moving general equilibrium a similar procedure may be followed. From a study of the simultaneous equations determining the moving general equilibrium the possible sources of oscillations may be located, whether these be in the amounts of consumable goods demanded, the quantities of productive services supplied, the degree of saving, the kinds and quantities of new capital goods manufactured, or the quantity of money in circulation. The complete theory of oscillations, like the complete theory of the quantity demanded of a single commodity, would be approached by successive approximations. A first approximation would take cognizance of the most important cause of perturbation, and the successive approximations would be made by combining the effects of the several perturbing causes.

But can these complex actions and reactions be followed up in reality? In mathematical physics there is a theory of oscillations developed by Daniel Bernouilli which presents a curious and inspiriting parallel to the problem before us. According to Bernouilli's theorem, a system in equilibrium tends, under the influence of a perturbing cause, to oscillate about its position of normal stability, and the partial oscillations that are due to different causes coexist in harmony with the general conditions determining the equilibrium. The successful application of this principle in different branches of mathematical physics should give courage to the synthetic economist.

CHAPTER II

FUNDAMENTAL NOTIONS

"En dépit de certaines apparences, l'ensemble de nos connaissances et de notre science est surtout pratique, subjectif, provisoire et convenu en sa définition, subordonné à son utilisation sociale."

ALFRED LOISY

The pure theory of economics rests upon an obscure premise; it employs certain concepts with a narrowly technical meaning; it gives two interpretations of facts according as a mathematical postulate is accepted or rejected; it has reached a point in its growth where, through an accumulation of hypotheses and postulates, the burden of presuppositions impedes its further progress. The object of the present chapter is to appraise these theoretical premises, concepts, postulates, and disabilities for the purpose of gaining a larger freedom in the constructive work of the ensuing chapters.

The Premise of Free Competition

One of the chief difficulties of economic theory is the bewildering vagueness of its fundamental premise. Competition is the fundamental hypothesis of the science in the sense that competition is postulated in nearly every argument concerned with the determination of prices. But what is the meaning of "perfect competition"? In what respect is the idea of "competition" changed by the addition of such modifiers as

11

"perfect," "unlimited," "indefinite," "free," "pure," "absolute"? If by these additions there is a change of meaning in the term, then, in cases in which the state of industry admits only of "competition," what is the nature of the limitation of propositions deduced on the hypothesis of "perfect competition"? This question is usually evaded by saying,—the imperfection of competition is simply a form of friction, producing for the most part a negligible variation from the standards prevailing in a regime of perfect competition. This complacent reply should be scrutinized. If one is inclined to accept it, what shall be said to the following statement by Pareto:

"La libre concurrence produit le maximum d'ophélimité; la libre concurrence règne dans nos sociétés: ce sont là deux propositions différentes. La première est très probablement vraie; la seconde est certainement fausse."[1]

Here is an authoritative statement that "free competition" does not reign in modern societies. Then where, precisely, is the limit of the applicability of propositions deduced by the *École de Lausanne* on the hypothesis of "free competition"? Is it allowable to infer, for example, that actual wages deviate only in a negligible way from the standard which would prevail under "free competition"? That is not the idea of Pareto:

"Il n'y a donc nulle contradiction entre la théorie qui assigne comme effet le maximum d'utilité à cette libre concurrence, et l'observation qui fait voir qu'un régime essentiellement différent produit une effroyable misère." "M. Bodio, le savant directeur

[1] Pareto: *Cours d'économie politique*. Vol. II, p. 130, note (788)².

de la statistique italienne, dit que la misère des classes agricoles italiennes atteint des limites absolument incroyables." [2] According to the theory of the *École de Lausanne* wages under "free competition" would reach a level at which there would be a maximum of satisfaction compatible with private property, whereas the actual state of Italian agricultural laborers, at the time in which Pareto wrote, was one of incredible wretchedness.

The word "competition," as used in economic theory, is a blanket-term covering more or less completely the following implicit hypotheses:

(*a*) Every economic factor seeks and obtains a maximum net income. This is the essential meaning of the term.[3] It is made the basis of the definition of the science given by Edgeworth: "Economics investigates the arrangements between agents each tending to his own maximum utility." [4] This aspect of competition is always explicitly emphasized in those

[2] Pareto: *Cours d'économie politique.* Vol. II, pp. 166 and 166, note (814)². Cf. also *ibid.*, Vol. II, p. 137, for a statement more in harmony with the current conception: "Nous avons supposé dans nos théories la concurrence parfaite, et nous avons insisté sur le fait que ce n'est là qu'un état limite. En réalité, la concurrence est souvent imparfaite, il se produit un effet analogue à celui des frottements dans les machines."

[3] "It is to Quesnay in his *Dialogues sur les travaux des artisans* that we owe the first, and very categorical enunciation of the formula which has been so famous under the name of the edonistic (?) principle, and constitutes, in fact, the basis of economics: 'To obtain the greatest possible increase of enjoyment with the greatest decrease of expense is the perfection of economics.' It is no exaggeration to say that he who enunciated this principle has indeed a right to the title of Founder of Economic Science." Gide's review of Higgs' *Physiocrats, Economic Journal*, June, 1897, p. 248.

[4] Edgeworth: *Mathematical Psychics*, p. 6.

systems of economics using analytical symbols, since it at once suggests, as Malthus foresaw, that "many of the questions, both in morals and politics, seem to be of the nature of problems *de maximis et minimis* in Fluxions." [5] It is the prime hypothesis used in Cournot's essay: "Nous n'invoquerons qu'un seul axiome, ou, si l'on veut, nous n'employerons qu'une seule hypothèse, savoir que chacun cherche à tirer de sa chose ou de son travail la plus grande valeur possible." [6] It may be called the maximum hypothesis of competition.

(*b*) There is but one price for commodities of the same quality in the same market. This is referred to by Jevons as the law of indifference, and it is constantly used as a premise in his theory of equilibrium. It is also used by Cournot, notwithstanding the above statement that he would invoke but a single axiom: "Il ne peut pas y avoir dans une ordre de chose stable, et sur une grande échelle, deux prix différents pour une même quantité débitée." [7] As an illustration of the identification of this hypothesis with competition, a passage from Jevons' *Principles of Economics*

[5] Malthus: *Observations on the Effects of the Corn Laws*, 1814, p. 30.

[6] Cournot: *Recherches sur les principes mathématiques de la théorie des richesses*, p. 46.

[7] *Ibid.*, p. 73.

may be cited: "This law of indifference, in fact, is but another name for the principle of competition which underlies the whole mechanism of society " (p. 60).

(c) The influence of the product of any one producer upon the price per unit of the total product is negligible. An illustration is found in Pareto's *Cours d'économie politique*, Vol. I, p. 20: "L'échangeur subit les prix du marché sans essayer de les modifier de propos délibéré. Ces prix sont modifiés effectivement par son offre et sa demande, mais c'est à son insu. *C'est ce qui caractérise l'état que nous appelons de libre concurrence*. . . . En langage mathématique nous dirons que pour établir les conditions du maximum, on différentie en supposant les prix constants." [8]

(d) The output of any one producer is negligible as compared with the total output. Marshall has discussed this assumption in Note xiv of the Appendix to his *Principles of Economics,* particularly p. 801 of the 4th edition.

(e) Each producer regulates the amount of his output without regard to the effect of his act upon the conduct of his competitors. Where (c) and (d) coexist, (e) is a simple corollary; otherwise, it is an independent and inadmissible hypothesis.

[8] One sentence in the quotation I have italicized in order to draw attention to Pareto's having definitely regarded this feature as the characteristic of "free competition."

In most systems of economics, a theory of exchange, production, and distribution is developed by reasoning consciously from hypotheses (a) and (e). It is not by any means always perceived, however, that the truth of the theory is further limited by the implicit assumption of hypotheses (c) and (d). This loose method of procedure entails no necessary harm so long as the investigation is confined to a simplified, hypothetical static state, but great harm is done when, in approaching the problems of actual industry—which, to a large extent, is in a state intermediate between perfect monopoly and perfect competition—the economist flings the inquirer into the vague with the assurance that theoretical standards will tend to prevail. In this intermediate state between perfect monopoly and perfect competition hypothesis (a) is, at best, only approximately true; hypothesis (b) is frequently untrue; and hypotheses (c) and (d), in many spheres, are never true.

In pure economic theory, when the assumption of "free competition" lies at the basis of the reasoning, all five of the above enumerated hypotheses are implicitly postulated. Here we come upon a principal cause of the gross conflict of theoretical conclusions and observed facts. "La libre concurrence produit le maximum d'ophélimité." "La misère des classes agricoles italiennes atteint des limites absolument incroyables" (Pareto). Obviously, some method must be devised for bringing theory into closer harmony with observed facts. In pure theory, the fundamental laws, for example the laws of demand and supply, are such as would obtain on the hypothesis of "free competition" in a static state. In Synthetic Economics, the fundamental laws are obtained directly from reality. The difference in the two superstructures is the difference between a purely formal science and a positive science.

Capitals and Services

A scientific classification, like a scientific method, is to be judged by its fitness for its purpose. In the historic treatment of capital and income much ability has been directed toward a definition of terms and an effort to bring them into a logical classification. But the goal of the great talents thus employed has not always been well defined, and without a distinct specification of the goal such dialectical endeavors might obviously be endlessly prolonged. The *École de Lausanne* has been exemplarily clear as to its aim. Its ultimate object has been to describe the ensemble of the interrelations in exchange, production, and capitalization, and with this object always in view it has defined and classified capitals and services.

With the work of the *École de Lausanne* as a point of departure in Synthetic Economics it is desirable, in the interest both of science and of personal loyalty, to adhere as far as possible not only to Walras' terms but also to his symbols. His terms are in some cases uncommon, but the use of them has been continued by his most distinguished disciples; his symbols, for the most part, have been retained, and where substitutes have been offered the innovations have seldom proved to be betterments.

Walras' classification of capitals and services may be summarized in the following scheme:

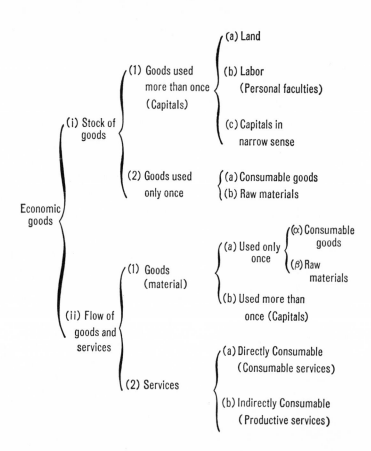

Anything that has *rareté* (marginal utility) is by that fact an economic good. These goods may be regarded from the point of view of a given epoch, or from the point of view of a flow of time. At any given epoch the stock of goods will be made up of those goods which afford more than one use and of those which are used only once. The former are called Capitals and are subdivided into land, labor (personal faculties), and capitals in the narrow sense; the latter are made up of consumers' goods and raw materials. Capitals in the narrow sense include all those goods that are used more than once and are neither land nor labor. This category embraces savings and money as well as commodities usually called capital goods.

With the passing of time there is a flow of material goods and services. The flow of material goods takes the form either of capitals or of consumers' goods and raw materials. The capital goods are either of the current types or of new types. The services are either productive services or directly consumable services.

The object of the classification, as has been said, is to describe the ensemble of interrelations in exchange, production, and capitalization. This problem of description is approached by successive approximations. In the theory of exchange those interrelations are considered which determine the prices of consumable material goods and directly consumable services. In the theory of production those supplementary interrelations which are required to determine the prices of raw materials and productive services are added; in the theory of capitalization the remaining conditions which are necessary to determine the prices of capital goods are introduced into the general system of equations.

Economic Equilibria

The idea of a social equilibrium is found, in germ, wherever the study of social science has been approached systematically. It appears in Greek speculation, in the thought of the schoolmen of the Middle Ages, in the theory of the Physiocrats, in the treatises of the classical economists. The germ idea of an economic equilibrium is simply that of a balance of the many forces operative upon a price configuration, which configuration, with respect to the balanced forces, remains in a state of rest. It received a marked and explicit development in the work of Cournot,[9] and has been made a fundamental notion in the treatises of the *École de Lausanne*. In the hands of these mathematical economists the notion is so carefully elaborated and so definitely linked with the whole of economic theory that it is virtually the means of a new conception of the science.[10]

This new conception of economic science we have sought to develop, starting with the following classification of equilibria:

[9] Cournot: *Researches into the Mathematical Principles of the Theory of Wealth.* Bacon's translation, p. 127. Cf. also Professor Umberto Ricci: "Non è che al Cournot mancasse una visione dell'equilibrio generale. Egli ebbe una nozione dell'equilibrio, per i suoi tempi assai ragguardevole." *Giornale degli Economisti*, Gennaio-Febbraio, 1924, p. 35.

[10] "Una delle scoperte più profonde a cui gli economisti letterari siano pervenuti in fatto di teorie concernenti l'equilibrio economico, consiste appunto nel rilievo che il concetto di equilibrio e di interdipendenza dei fatti economici non è poi tanto nuovo, esso ritrovandosi in fondo anche presso molti economisti classici, specialmente in J. B. Say. Quasichè sia la stessa cosa accennare più o meno di sfuggita, e male, ad un concetto, ovvero precisarlo matematicamente, trasformandolo poi in una base nuova ed estremamente feconda di studio di tutto un gruppo di fatti!" Guido Sensini: *La Teoria della Rendita*, p. 311, note.

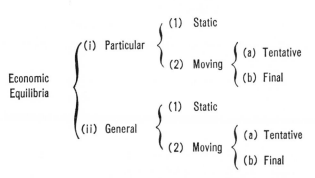

The equilibrium may refer either to a single commodity or to the whole economic system. The former is a particular equilibrium; the latter, a general equilibrium. Either of these may be either static or moving, and a moving equilibrium, whether particular or general, may be either tentative or final.

The key to the distinction between tentative and final moving equilibria lies in the flow of time. In case of a particular commodity the distinction is similar to that between market price and normal price. The classical discrimination between market price and normal price is directed toward an understanding of the effect upon price of forces which take time to be brought into play. The market price is not directly affected by the cost of production but is determined by the law of demand and the quantity of commodity that is put upon the market. There is a *tentative* equilibrium of demand and supply which determines the market price. But if the market price exceeds, or falls short of, the cost of production, forces are brought into play which, theoretically, will lead to such a readjustment of the supply that the resultant price, the normal price, will afford a *final* equilibrium. Demand

and supply will then be equated at a price which will offer no inducement to change any factor in the equilibrium.

In case of the general economic system the distinction between tentative and final moving equilibria is also analogous to that between market price and normal price, and is likewise traceable to the flow of time. In a definite time, say a particular year, the economic organism brings to fruition many consumable commodities and consumable services. For the time being the prices of these are determined by the existing laws of demand for the commodities and services, and the quantities of services and commodities put upon the markets. In the determination of the prices, cognizance is taken of the whole complex of commodities and services and their respective laws of demand, but little or no attention is paid to what the costs of production may have been. The resulting prices are prices at *tentative* equilibria. These tentative equilibria involve profits or losses arising out of the differences between prices and costs of production, and these profits and losses become spurs to economic readjustments. The magnitude of the readjustments is again a question of the flow of time. It takes time to make a readjustment with the existing machinery of production, and it takes a still longer time to make a readjustment involving the saving of capital and the creation of new machinery. If the readjustment is made with the existing technical equipment, there may be other *tentative* equilibria where demand and supply are balanced but where prices and costs are at variance. Readjustment will now be made by altering the instruments of production, and, if there are no new perturbations, will proceed until a stage is reached in which not only demand and supply with reference to all commodities and services are balanced, but costs of production and market prices are, likewise, equated. Equilibrium will then exist throughout the whole economic system, and the equilibrium will be *final* because there will be no inducement to alter any factor in the equilibrium.

This series of readjustments has been described on the supposition that no new perturbation occurs. But new perturbations always do occur, and, consequently, the final equilibria become shifting ideal goals whose lines of motion trace out the *trends* of the system of economic quantities. Perturbations of final equilibria start the changes whose immediate goals are tentative equilibria; but the occurrence, or prospect, of new perturbations disturbs the immediate adjustment of the results of earlier changes, with the consequence that the tentative equilibria likewise become ideal goals, whose lines of motion trace out the *oscillations* about the trends of final equilibria.

The Postulate of the Negligibility of Indirect Effects

In an early stage of economic speculation there was a dim perception that a clue to the understanding of the oscillatory character of economic changes could be found in demand and supply. Indeed, the terms demand and supply were vaguely used as summary names for the groups of forces whose opposed working produced the oscillatory course of economic changes. With the advance of economic theory it became necessary to give, first, an abstract, then, a concrete formulation of the laws of demand and supply. For theoretical purposes it does not suffice to refer vaguely to the laws of demand and supply as being responsible for observed changes; one must know the general mathematical character of the function descriptive of demand and the function descriptive of supply. For more exacting, concrete, practical purposes, the parameters in the functions descriptive of the laws must be deduced in numerical form from actual observations.

But how shall the investigator proceed to formulate these laws abstractly, then concretely?

Looking back over the history of economic theory, we see that the formulation has varied according as the investigator has, or has not, made use of the hypothesis of the negligibility of indirect effects. The root idea of this postulate has been described in general terms by Marshall:

"It was not till the seventeenth century that the physical sciences appreciated the full importance of the fact that when several causes act together and mutually affect one another, then each cause produces two classes of effects: those which are direct, and those which result indirectly from the influence exerted by it on other causes: for indeed these direct and indirect effects are apt to become so intricately interwoven that they can by no means be disentangled. So far the results are negative: they seem to indicate that the task of following out and understanding the combined action of several causes, which are in various degrees mutually interdependent, is beyond the power of human faculty. But a way out of the difficulty was found, chiefly under the guidance of Leibnitz and

Newton. An epoch-making process of reasoning showed that, though the indirect effects might grow cumulatively, and ere long become considerable, yet at first they would be very small indeed relatively to the direct effects. Hence it was concluded that a study of the tendency to change, resulting from each several disturbing cause, might be made the starting point for a broad study of the influence of several causes acting together. This principle is the foundation of the victory of analytical methods in many fields of science. Its best known triumph is that of the Nautical Almanack which takes into account the disturbing influences exerted by any two planets on one another directly, and also indirectly as the result of their disturbances of other planets." [11]

It would not be difficult to show that Marshall constructed his *Principles of Economics*, from beginning to end, upon this method of analysis. Our misfortune is that he followed the method only through the first stage. His laws of demand and supply are laws of the variation of demand price and supply price with the variation of the quantity of commodity, on the hypothesis that all other things remain equal. The indirect effects of the variation of any one commodity upon the prices of other commodities are neglected.

There is a principle of research in chemistry the purport of which is in this precept—if you want to make discoveries, look to your residues. Marshall's practice in his *Principles* has been to invoke systematically the postulate of the negligibility of indirect effects. What discovery shall we make if we examine

[11] Marshall: *Industry and Trade*, pp. 677–678.

the discarded residue? Nothing less, as we shall see, than the explanation of general economic oscillations. The postulate described above in general terms by Marshall has also been employed by Cournot, whose description of his particular problem shows the truth of the statement which has just been made, that the discarded residue of indirect effects contains the explanation of general economic oscillations:

"In general . . . it must be the case, that a perturbation experienced by one element of the system (of prices) makes itself felt from that to the next, and by reaction throughout the entire system. Nevertheless, since the variation occurring in the price of commodity *A*, and in the income of its producers, leaves intact the sum total of the funds applicable to the demand for the other commodities, *B, C, D, E*, etc., it is evident that the sum diverted, by hypothesis, from commodity *B*, by reason of the new direction of demands, will necessarily be applied to the demand for one or several of the commodities *C, D, E*, etc. *Strictly speaking, this perturbation of the second degree, which occurs in the incomes of the producers of B, C, D, etc., would react on the system in turn until a new equilibrium is established; but, although we are unable to calculate this series of reactions, the general principles of analysis will show us that they must go on with gradually decreasing amplitude,* so that it may be admitted, as an approximation, that a variation occurring in the incomes of the producers of *A*, while modifying the distribution of the remainder of the social income among the producers of *B, C, D, E*, etc., does not alter the total value of it, or only alters it by a quantity which is negligible in comparison with the variation which is experienced by the incomes of producers of A."[12]

In the preceding quotation the words I have italicized contain the expression "a new equilibrium" ("un nouvel équilibre"); also the germ-idea of a general equilibrium, the conception of oscillations about the equilibrium, and the explicit statement that "the general principles of analysis will show us that they (the reactions) must go on with gradually decreasing amplitude." When an economic system is in equilibrium any perturbation, according to Cournot, will set up primary or direct effects, which are limited to the immediate object disturbed, and secondary or indirect effects, which result from the *liaisons* between all the elements in the system. In consequence of these functional *liaisons*, the indirect effects are diffused throughout the entire system in the form of oscillations which "the general principles of analysis will show us must go on with gradually decreasing amplitude." Neglect of the indirect effects obviously involves the neglect of the phenomena and mechanism of general economic oscillations.

If one employs the postulate of the negligibility of indirect effects, a first approximation to the laws of demand and supply may be obtained by representing both demand and supply as functions of a single variable. This is the course followed by Cournot and Marshall. If, on the other hand, one aspires to explain general economic equilibria and to follow out the oscillations about the general equilibria, the *liaisons*

[12] Cournot: *Researches into the Mathematical Principles of the Theory of Wealth*. Bacon's translation, § 76, pp. 130–131

among all the elements of the systems must be known, and the indirect effects of perturbations become the conditions of the explanation of oscillations. The point of departure for this undertaking is to represent demand and supply not as functions of a single price but as functions of all prices. This is the course followed by Léon Walras and his disciples of the *École de Lausanne*.

Obsolescent Disabilities

A discerning critic, Professor Umberto Ricci, has summarily appraised the work of the *École de Lausanne*. As late as 1924 he expressed the following opinion: "After due acknowledgment has been made to the authors of one of the most wonderful creations of human thought, one cannot but circumscribe the field of its application. The whole construction gives the effect of an enchanted palace which delights the fantasy but does not help to solve problems of housing. Or, to drop the metaphor, the theory remains abstract and intangible." [13] In particular, Professor Ricci remarks that there is no bridge between the pure theory of Pareto and nine-tenths of the problems with which the economist is usually concerned. He asks whether the bridge between theory and fact may yet be built after mathematical knowledge shall have progressed beyond its present stage and statistical

[13] "Ma tutto questo riconosciuto, e tributata la dovuta riconoscenza agli autori di una delle più meravigliose creazioni del pensiero umano, non si può non circoscrivere di questa il campo di applicazione.

"Tutta la costruzione fa un po' l'effetto di un castello incantata che bea la fantasia, ma non aiuta a risolvere il problema degli alloggi. Ossia, per uscir di metafora, la teoria rimane astratta e inafferrabile." *Giornale degli Economisti*, Gennaio–Febbraio, 1924, p. 43.

data shall have become more numerous, and he replies to his own question with the non-committal words: Let us hope so. It cannot be denied that his views are shared by many well-informed scholars. But what is the source of the sense of unreality so many experience after having heroically struggled through the writings of Walras and Pareto? What is the prospect not only of removing from the theory of equilibrium the sources of unreality but of utilizing, in a practical manner, a theoretical scheme of thought which embraces the ensemble of interrelated phenomena?

Foremost among the causes of the sense of unreality are these: the method of proceeding by successive approximations in the approach to a theory of general equilibrium, which gives a feeling of an indefinitely postponed real solution; the use of the hypothesis of perfect competition with a meaning which does not accord with reality; the limitation of all conclusions to a static state, when, as a matter of fact, all economic phenomena are in a perpetual flux; the assumption of an immediate adjustment of changes, when in reality there are always lags and leads; the complexity of the functions that must be derived from reality and the absence of any known method of making the derivation; the assumption that the simultaneous equations can never be solved, first, because their empirical forms can never be known, and secondly, if they were known, their great number would preclude the possibility of their solution. There may be other reasons, but those enumerated are certainly sufficient to account for the sense of unreality.

Every one of these disabilities may be mitigated, if not entirely removed.

With regard to the method of successive approximations, a distinction should be made between the successive approximations which have been traversed in the historic development of a theory and the successive approximations in the accuracy with which a known theory may be made to describe reality. Walras began his work with the theory of utility and made the conduct of the individual his point of departure. Working in an uncharted region he observed all the caution necessary to safeguard every step, being content if each stage seemed to bring him nearer his goal of a comprehensive view of social conduct. When at last he reached the abstract simultaneous equations descriptive of social behavior, the long laborious process by which the results were achieved became, primarily, of historic interest, but the abstract equations may now be given a real form and may be made to yield, by successive approximations, an increasingly accurate description of reality.

The manner of circumventing the difficulties of the hypothesis of perfect competition will be treated in Chapter V, on "Moving Equilibria."

Two other causes of the sense of unreality in the work of the *École de Lausanne*—the limitation of the results to an hypothetical static state, and the absence of any known method of deriving the necessary empirical equations from reality—disappear with the actual derivation of these equations for a perpetually changing state. Moreover, once we are in possession of the concrete functions, it is not only unnecessary to make the assumption of immediate adjustment of economic changes, but the real lags and leads themselves become the foundation of a realistic theory of economic oscillations about the general equilibria. Of the enumerated sources of the sense of unreality there remains the assumption that the simultaneous equations can never be solved, first, because their empirical forms can never be known, and secondly, if they were known, their great number would preclude the possibility of their solution.[14] The first part of this assumption, that the empirical forms of the equations

[14] "Les conditions que nous avons énumérées pour l'équilibre économique nous donnent une notion générale de cet équilibre. Pour savoir ce qu'étaient certains phénomènes nous avons dû étudier leur manifestations; pour savoir ce que c'était que l'équilibre économique, nous avons dû rechercher comment il était déterminé. Remarquons, d'ailleurs, que cette détermination n'a nullement pour but d'arriver à un calcul numérique des prix. Faisons l'hypothèse la plus favorable à un tel calcul; supposons que nous ayons triomphé de toutes les difficultés pour arriver à connaître les données du problème, et que nous connaissions les ophélimités de toutes les marchandises pour chaque individu, toutes les circonstances de la production des marchandises, etc. C'est là déjà une hypothèse absurde, et pourtant elle ne nous donne pas encore la possibilité pratique de résoudre ce problème. Nous avons vu que dans le cas de 100 individus et de 700 marchandises il y aurait 70,699 conditions (en réalité un grand nombre de circonstances, que nous avons jusqu'ici négligées, augmenteraient encore ce nombre); nous aurons donc à résoudre un système de 70,699 équations. Cela dépasse pratiquement la puissance de l'analyse de l'analyse algébrique, et cela la dépasserait encore davantage si l'on prenait en considération le nombre fabuleux d'équations que donnerait une population de quarante millions d'individus, et quelques milliers de marchandises. Dans ce cas les rôles seraient changés: et ce ne seraient plus les mathématiques qui viendraient en aide à l'économie politique, mais l'économie politique qui viendrait en aide aux mathématiques. En d'autres termes, si on pouvait vraiment connaître toutes ces équations, le seul moyen accessible aux forces humaines pour les résoudre, ce serait d'observer la solution pratique que donne le marché." Pareto: *Manuel d'économie politique*, pp. 233–234.

can never be known, is, of course, erroneous if we actually do derive the necessary concrete functions. The second part of the assumption—that the great number of the equations, even if known, would preclude the possibility of their solution—seems to be a serious, if not a fatal, disability. If the equations can not be solved it might seem necessary to infer that the equilibria values can never be known, and in this case the whole theory of economic equilibria must forever remain an unverifiable speculation. But, fortunately, it would be an error to make such an inference. The equilibria values may be known without solving the equations. The method of deriving the empirical functions suggests a way of guessing the equilibria values, and the guessed values satisfy the system of simultaneous equations.

The ensemble of economic interrelations may be described concretely in their perpetual flux.

CHAPTER III

THE LAW OF DEMAND

"Kann man nicht die Nachfragefunktion genauer festellen, so genau, dass wir nicht bloss ein eindeutiges, sondern ein konkretes Resultat gewinnen? Ich glaube die Antwort zu hören: Welch' ein phantastisches Unterfangen—Unberechenbarkeit der wirtschaftlichen Vorgänge—steter Wechsel—u.s.w.!"

JOSEPH SCHUMPETER

Effective use of mathematical methods in the elucidation of economic theory was begun by Cournot in his treatment of the law of demand. The same law has been more amply investigated in the researches of his mathematical successors, and, because of its critical importance, will, with the law of supply, occupy a principal place in Synthetic Economics. The statistical methods which prove adequate to the concrete presentation of the law of demand will serve also to clothe with reality the law of supply. The theory of demand will be presented in this chapter and will be followed in the next with the theory of supply.

Elasticity of Demand and Flexibility of Prices

The quantitative treatment of the conception that lies at the basis of elasticity of demand originated with Cournot. Marshall gave the conception a name and simplified and extended its presentation.

According to Cournot, if $D = F(p)$ is the symbolic expression of the relation between the quantity of commodity demanded, D, and the price per unit of

33

commodity, p, then for many problems in economics it is of importance to know for what value of p the product $pF(p)$ is a maximum. One of Cournot's concrete illustrations is that of a monopolist, owning a mineral spring where the cost of production is negligible, who wishes to know what price of the commodity will yield him the largest monopoly return. The mathematical condition of a maximum return is

$$\frac{d[pF(p)]}{dp} = F(p) + pF'(p) = 0. \qquad (1)$$

The root of equation (1) is the price that will afford the maximum profit. In order to carry this problem to a concrete solution we must know the empirical form of $D = F(p)$. Upon this statistical problem Cournot makes the following comment:

"We may admit that it is impossible to determine the function $F(p)$ empirically for each article, but it is by no means the case that the same obstacles prevent the approximate determination of the value of p which satisfies equation (1) or which renders the product $pF(p)$ a maximum. *The construction of a table, where these values could be found, would be the work best calculated for preparing for the practical and rigorous solution of questions relating to the theory of wealth.*

"But even if it were impossible to obtain from statistics the value of p which should render $pF(p)$ a maximum, it would be easy to learn, at least for all articles to which the attempt has been made to extend commercial statistics, whether current prices are above or below this value. Suppose that when the price becomes $p + \Delta p$ the annual consumption as shown by statistics . . . becomes $D - \Delta D$. According as $\Delta D/\Delta p <$ or $> D/p$, the increase in price, Δp, will increase or diminish the product $pF(p)$; and, consequently, it will be known whether the two values p and $p + \Delta p$ (assuming Δp to be a small fraction of p) fall above or below the value which makes the product under consideration a maximum.[1]

"Commercial statistics should therefore be required to separate articles of high economic importance into two categories, according as their current prices are above or below the value which makes a maximum of $pF(p)$. We shall see that *many economic problems have different solutions, according as the article in question belongs to one or the other of these two categories.*"[2]

Some of Cournot's statements in the preceding quotation have been italicized to indicate that, in his opinion, we must know the empirical laws of demand

[1] The method of reaching the inequality discussed in the text may be indicated:

The increase in price will increase the gross receipts if

$$(p + \Delta p)(D - \Delta D) > pD,$$

or

$$pD - p \cdot \Delta D + D \cdot \Delta p - \Delta p \cdot \Delta D > pD,$$

or

$$- p \cdot \Delta D + D \cdot \Delta p - \Delta p \cdot \Delta D > 0,$$

or

$$\Delta D(p + \Delta p) < D \cdot \Delta p,$$

or

$$\frac{\Delta D}{\Delta p} < \frac{D}{p + \Delta p},$$

or, when Δp is small as compared with p,

$$\frac{\Delta D}{\Delta p} < \frac{D}{p}.$$

[2] Cournot: *Researches into the Mathematical Principles of the Theory of Wealth*, Bacon's translation, pp. 53–54.

for commodities if we are to pass to the practical and rigorous solution of questions relating to the theory of wealth.

The classification that Cournot makes between commodities according as $\Delta D/\Delta p <$ or $> D/p$ is essentially the classification which has subsequently been made to distinguish between inelastic and elastic commodities, flexible and inflexible prices. To show this let us pass from Cournot's symbols to those that have been rendered more familiar by Marshall. In Marshall's notation, x stands for the quantity demanded, and y, for the price per unit of commodity. If we substitute these symbols for those of Cournot, we may write Cournot's statement in this way: According as $\Delta x/\Delta y <$ or $> x/y$, the increase in price,

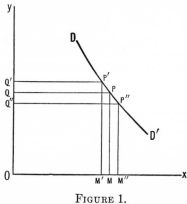

FIGURE 1.

Δy, will increase or diminish the product xy.

So far Cournot carried the problem. But his statement may be easily simplified and its economic significance rendered much clearer. In Figure 1 we have the familiar graph of the law of demand, where $x =$ the quantity of commodity demanded; $y =$ the price per unit of commodity; and DD' is the demand curve. Let the quantity actually demanded be $x = OM$, and the resulting actual price be $y = MP$. Then, in agreement with Cournot's formula, it would be profitable to the monopolist to raise or lower his price according as

$$\frac{\Delta x}{\Delta y} < \text{ or } > \frac{x}{y}. \qquad (2)$$

The inequality (2) may be divided through either by x/y or by $\Delta x/\Delta y$. If we divide through by x/y, we get

$$\frac{\Delta x}{\Delta y} \cdot \frac{y}{x} < \text{ or } > 1, \qquad (3)$$

which is Marshall's form of statement. He regards $\Delta x/\Delta y \cdot y/x$ as the measure of the elasticity of demand and describes the demand for the commodity as inelastic or elastic according as $\Delta x/\Delta y \cdot y/x$ is numerically less or greater than unity. If we call $dx/dy \cdot y/x$ the coefficient of elasticity of demand and indicate it by η, we may state Cournot's proposition as follows: The gross receipts of a monopolist will be increased or diminished by an increase of price according as $-\eta < \text{ or } > 1$; that is, according as the demand for the commodity is inelastic or elastic. This form of expression we have reached by dividing Cournot's inequality (2) by x/y.

But we might have divided it by $\Delta x/\Delta y$. If we do so now, we shall have

$$1 < \text{ or } > \frac{x}{y} \cdot \frac{\Delta y}{\Delta x}. \qquad (4)$$

Let us call $dy/dx \cdot x/y$ the coefficient of flexibility of price and indicate it by ϕ. Cournot's proposition would then be as follows: The gross receipts of a monopolist will be increased or diminished by an increase in price according as $-\phi >$ or < 1; that is, according as the price is flexible or inflexible.

Returning now to the use of Cournot's symbols, we may give formal definitions of elasticity of demand and flexibility of price. If η be taken as the symbol to represent elasticity of demand, and if $p =$ the price per unit of commodity and $D =$ the quantity of commodity demanded at price p, the elasticity of demand is

$$\eta = \frac{dD}{D} \bigg/ \frac{dp}{p} = \frac{p}{D} \cdot \frac{dD}{dp}. \tag{5}$$

Elasticity of demand is then defined as the ratio of the relative change in the quantity of commodity demanded to the relative change in the price per unit of commodity. When η is numerically greater than unity, the demand for the commodity is said to be elastic; when η is numerically less than unity, the demand is inelastic.

Similarly, if ϕ is taken as the symbol to represent flexibility of price, the definition of flexibility becomes

$$\phi = \frac{dp}{p} \bigg/ \frac{dD}{D} = \frac{D}{p} \cdot \frac{dp}{dD}. \tag{6}$$

That is to say, flexibility of price is the ratio of the relative change in price to the relative change in the quantity of commodity demanded. When ϕ is numerically greater than unity, the price is said to be flexible; when ϕ is numerically less than unity, price is inflexible.

Typical Demand Functions of One Variable

We have been taught by Cournot—and the work of Marshall has impressed the lesson—that the solution

of many problems in economics turns upon the
character of what has been defined as elasticity of
demand, or flexibility of price. Quite obviously, therefore, it is highly desirable to find typical demand
functions whose parameters reveal the character either
of elasticity of demand or of flexibility of price. This
practical need suggests the method to follow in de-
ducing equations of demand curves. If the quantity
of commodity put upon the market is taken as the
independent variable, increasingly complex demand
functions may be derived by integrating the differential equations obtained by putting

$$\phi = \begin{cases} \alpha, \text{ or} \\ \alpha + \alpha'D, \text{ or} \\ \alpha + \alpha'D + \alpha''D^2. \end{cases}$$

In these equations, ϕ is the flexibility of price, and,
according to the preceding paragraph,

$$\phi = \frac{dp}{p} \bigg/ \frac{dD}{D},$$

where $D =$ the quantity of commodity demanded,
and p is the price per unit of commodity. The first
assumption made in the above differential equations is
that the flexibility of price is a constant; the next
assumption is that the flexibility of price is a linear
function of the quantity of commodity demanded;
the third assumption is that flexibility is a quadratic
function of the quantity demanded.

If the flexibility of price is assumed to be constant, we have

$$\phi = \frac{dp}{p} \Big/ \frac{dD}{D} = \alpha,$$

or

$$\frac{dp}{p} = \alpha \frac{dD}{D}.$$

Integrating, we get

$$\log_e p = \alpha \log_e D + \log_e A.$$

Or, passing from logarithms to absolute numbers, we obtain as the typical demand function

$$p = AD^{\alpha}. \tag{7}$$

In this formula, A is the constant of integration to be determined from the observations.

If the flexibility of price is assumed to be a simple linear function of the quantity of commodity demanded, the differential equation is

$$\phi = \frac{dp}{p} \Big/ \frac{dD}{D} = \alpha + \alpha' D,$$

or

$$\frac{dp}{p} = \alpha \frac{dD}{D} + \alpha' dD,$$

which, when integrated, yields the typical demand function

$$p = AD^{\alpha} e^{\alpha' D}. \tag{8}$$

In this formula, e is the base of natural logarithms.

The third assumption,

$$\phi = \frac{dp}{p} \Big/ \frac{dD}{D} = \alpha + \alpha' D + \alpha'' D^2,$$

leads to the typical demand function,

$$p = AD^\alpha e^{\alpha'D + \frac{1}{2}\alpha''D^2}. \tag{9}$$

The typical demand functions (7, 8, 9) have been obtained by taking the quantity of commodity demanded as the independent variable, and starting with three simple assumptions with regard to the character of flexibility of price. If price is taken as the independent variable, we shall obtain other typical demand functions by starting with corresponding assumptions with regard to elasticity of demand. We may put

$$\eta = \frac{dD}{D} \Big/ \frac{dp}{p} = \begin{cases} \beta, \text{ or} \\ \beta + \beta'p, \text{ or} \\ \beta + \beta'p + \beta''p^2. \end{cases}$$

From these equations we obtain, by integrating, the typical demand functions,

$$D = Bp^\beta; \tag{10}$$

$$D = Bp^\beta e^{\beta'p}; \tag{11}$$

$$D = Bp^\beta e^{\beta'p + \frac{1}{2}\beta''p^2}. \tag{12}$$

In these equations, the B's are constants of integration, and e is the base of natural logarithms.

Statistical Derivation of Typical Demand Functions of One Variable

The preceding section gives useful forms of demand functions, and the present problem is to derive from observations the values of the parameters in those typical equations. The great difficulty in the undertaking lies in the fact that both prices and quantities of commodities are in a state of constant secular change. Several methods for overcoming this difficulty have been devised,[3] but in the subsequent reasoning use will be made only of the method of trend-ratios.

In preparing the data of prices and of quantities of commodities so that they may be used to deduce the law of demand by the method of trend-ratios, the prices of the commodity at successive points in time are expressed as ratios to the corresponding trends at the respective points in time. Similarly the quantities of commodity at the points in time are expressed as ratios to the corresponding commodity trends.

The general formula for the law of demand according to the method of trend-ratios is either

$$\frac{D}{\overline{D}} = F\left(\frac{p}{\overline{p}}\right), \tag{13}$$

where $\overline{D}$ is the trend of the quantity demanded at the particular time, and $\overline{p}$ is the trend of the corresponding price at the same time; or, if the quantity of commodity is taken as the independent variable,

$$\frac{p}{\overline{p}} = f\left(\frac{D}{\overline{D}}\right). \tag{14}$$

To find the concrete laws of demand, the general equation (13) may be taken in any one of the three forms (10, 11, 12), or the general equation (14) may be taken in any one of the forms (7, 8, 9).

[3] Henry Schultz: "The Statistical Law of Demand," *Journal of Political Economy*, October and December, 1925.

The steps in the statistical procedure will be illustrated by fitting typical equation (8) to data.

The *Yearbook of the Department of Agriculture* gives statistics of the production of agricultural commodities and of their respective prices throughout a long interval. The data referring to the production and prices of potatoes from 1881 to 1913 will be used to illustrate the derivation of the empirical law of demand for potatoes and the law of the flexibility of potato prices.

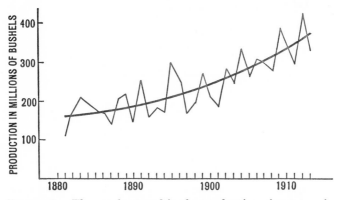

FIGURE 2.   The secular trend in the production of potatoes in the United States.

$y = 222.3 + 5.711t + .1758t^2 + .004363t^3$, origin at 1897.

In Figure 2 the secular trend of the production of potatoes from 1881 to 1913 is graphed, and a similar curve for the secular trend of prices of potatoes might be given.   The equation to the trend of production is printed on Figure 2; the equation to the trend of prices is, with origin at 1897.

$$p = 48.86 + 0.775t + 0.0443t^2 - 0.002935t^3.$$

TABLE I

THE ANNUAL PRODUCTION OF POTATOES AND THEIR DECEMBER FARM
PRICES IN THE UNITED STATES. PRODUCTION RATIOS AND
PRICE RATIOS

Year	Production: millions of bushels D	Price: cents per bushel p	Production ratio $D/\bar{D}$	Price ratio $p/\bar{p}$
1881..........	109	91.0	.690	1.52
82..........	171	55.7	1.062	.97
83..........	208	42.2	1.261	.77
84..........	191	39.6	1.137	.74
85..........	175	44.7	1.023	.88
86..........	168	46.7	.960	.94
87..........	134	68.2	.753	1.41
88..........	202	40.2	1.110	.85
89..........	218	35.4	1.172	.75
1890..........	148	75.8	.783	1.63
91..........	254	35.8	1.316	.76
92..........	157	66.1	.793	1.41
93..........	183	59.4	.906	1.27
94..........	171	53.6	.826	1.13
95..........	297	26.6	1.401	.56
96..........	252	28.6	1.161	.59
97..........	164	54.7	.739	1.12
98..........	192	41.4	.842	.84
99..........	273	39.0	1.162	.77
1900..........	211	43.1	.876	.84
01..........	188	76.7	.758	1.46
02..........	285	47.1	1.113	.88
03..........	247	61.4	.936	1.13
04..........	333	45.3	1.224	.82
05..........	261	61.7	.929	1.09
06..........	308	51.1	1.058	.89
07..........	298	61.8	.990	1.06
08..........	279	70.6	.894	1.21
09..........	389	54.1	1.201	.90
1910..........	349	55.7	1.039	.93
11..........	293	79.9	.840	1.33
12..........	421	50.5	1.163	.83
13..........	332	68.7	.883	1.14
Total..........			33.001	33.42
Mean..........			1.00	1.01

After the trends of the two series of figures—production and prices—have been computed, the next step in the problem is to express the observed values of the quantities as ratios to the corresponding respective trends. The ratios relating to production and prices we shall refer to, respectively, as production-ratios and price-ratios. In Table I these ratios are tabulated.

The correlation of the price-ratios and the production-ratios of potatoes is $r = -0.84$, which is sufficient evidence of a very high relation between the two series. Suppose, now, that the law of demand is of type (8). We should then be required to fit to the trend-ratios the formula

$$\frac{p}{\bar{p}} = A \left(\frac{D}{\bar{D}} \right)^\alpha e^{\alpha'(D/\bar{D})}. \tag{15}$$

Before proceeding to fit (15) to the data, we may effect a simplification by observing that the value of A is already known. When the price-ratio $p/\bar{p}$ is 1.0, the production ratio is likewise 1.0; and if these values [4] are substituted in (15), the value of A is found to be $e^{-\alpha'}$, and consequently (15) becomes

$$\frac{p}{\bar{p}} = \left(\frac{D}{\bar{D}} \right)^\alpha e^{\alpha'\left(\frac{D}{\bar{D}}-1\right)}. \tag{16}$$

To fit equation (16) to the observations, let us first take logarithms of both sides of the equation. We have

$$\log \left(\frac{p}{\bar{p}} \right) = \alpha \log \left(\frac{D}{\bar{D}} \right) + \alpha' \left(\frac{D}{\bar{D}} - 1 \right) \log e. \tag{17}$$

[4] In the particular case of potatoes the mean values of $D/\bar{D}$, $p/\bar{p}$ are, practically, 1.0. See Table I. There may be cases where it would be better not to use this hypothesis but to determine A from the observations. This could be done by following the same method as that described in the text.

If the method of least squares is used to fit (17) to the n observations, we have as the observation equations

$$\left[\log\left(\frac{p_1}{\bar{p}_1}\right) - \alpha \log\left(\frac{D_1}{\bar{D}_1}\right) - \alpha'\left(\frac{D_1}{\bar{D}_1} - 1\right)\log e \right]^2 = v_1{}^2,$$

$$\cdot \quad \cdot \quad \cdot \quad \cdot \quad \cdot \quad \cdot \quad \cdot \quad \cdot \quad \cdot \quad \cdot \quad \cdot \quad \cdot \quad \cdot \quad \cdot \quad \cdot$$

$$\left[\log\left(\frac{p_n}{\bar{p}_n}\right) - \alpha \log\left(\frac{D_n}{\bar{D}_n}\right) - \alpha'\left(\frac{D_n}{\bar{D}_n} - 1\right)\log e \right]^2 = v_n{}^2.$$

The sum of the squares of the errors, $\Sigma(v^2)$, is a function of α, α', and, in order to find their most probable values, we have the normal equations

$$\frac{\partial \Sigma v^2}{\partial \alpha} = \Sigma\left(\log\frac{p}{\bar{p}} \cdot \log\frac{D}{\bar{D}} \right) - \alpha\Sigma\left(\log\frac{D}{\bar{D}} \right)^2$$

$$- 0.4343\alpha'\Sigma\left(\frac{D}{\bar{D}}\log\frac{D}{\bar{D}} \right)$$

$$+ 0.4343\alpha'\Sigma\left(\log\frac{D}{\bar{D}} \right) = 0;$$

$$\frac{\partial \Sigma v^2}{\partial \alpha'} = \Sigma\left(\frac{D}{\bar{D}}\log\frac{p}{\bar{p}} \right) - \Sigma\left(\log\frac{p}{\bar{p}} \right) - \alpha\Sigma\left(\frac{D}{\bar{D}}\log\frac{D}{\bar{D}} \right)$$

$$+ \alpha\Sigma\left(\log\frac{D}{\bar{D}} \right) - 0.4343\alpha'\Sigma\left(\frac{D}{\bar{D}} \right)^2$$

$$+ 0.8686\alpha'\Sigma\left(\frac{D}{\bar{D}} \right) - 0.4343n\alpha' = 0.$$

By means of these two normal equations the most probable values of α and α' may be determined from the observations. When the calculation is carried out for the production-ratios and price-ratios of potatoes, the equation connecting the two is found to be

$$\frac{p}{\bar{p}} = \left(\frac{D}{\bar{\bar{D}}}\right)^{0.143} e^{-1.376\left(\frac{D}{\bar{D}}-1\right)}. \qquad (18)$$

Its graph is traced in Figure 3.

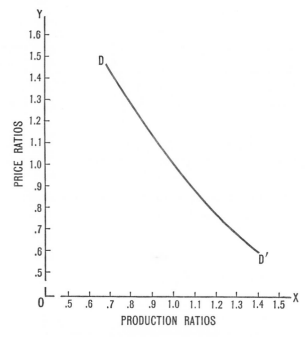

FIGURE 3. The law of demand for potatoes.

$$\frac{p}{\bar{p}} = \left(\frac{D}{\bar{\bar{D}}}\right)^{0.143} e^{-1.376\,[(D/\bar{D})-1]}.$$

Equation (18) gives the relation between the price-ratios and production-ratios for the interval 1881–1913. It may be called the law of demand for potatoes in the ratio form. By an obvious transformation of (18), the law of demand for any one year may be obtained in terms of absolute quantities. It is

$$p = \left\{ \frac{\overline{p}}{(\overline{D})^{0.143}} e^{1.376} \right\} D^{0.143} e^{-1.376(D/\overline{D})}$$

$$= AD^{0.143} e^{-1.376(D/\overline{D})}, \tag{19}$$

where

$$A = \left\{ \frac{\overline{p}}{(\overline{D})^{0.143}} e^{1.376} \right\}.$$

If, for example, the law of demand for potatoes in 1913 is to be ascertained, find the trend of prices for 1913, $\overline{p}$, and the trend of production for 1913, $\overline{D}$, and substitute these values in (19). The values of $\overline{p}$, $\overline{D}$ may be obtained for any one year from the equations to the trends which have already been given.[5]

The preceding derivation of the demand function also solves the problem of the law of variation of flexibility of price. By comparing the typical equation of demand (15) with the concrete equation of demand in ratio form (18) and with the demand equation in absolute form (19), we see that, in this particular case, the flexibility of price is

$$\phi = \alpha + \alpha' \left(\frac{D}{\overline{D}} \right) = 0.143 - 1.376 \left(\frac{D}{\overline{D}} \right).$$

[5] The objection may be made that, since the trends are described by parabolas of the type $y = a_0 + a_1 t + a_2 t^2 + a_3 t^3$, if we extrapolate for many years beyond the observations the curves may give impossible results. But the subject of the present discussion is not what will occur many years beyond the limits of observation. To a similar objection on the part of an unfriendly critic Pareto once replied: *Quando vi si dà una formula valevole entro certi limiti, chi vi insegna ad applicarla fuori di quei limiti?*

I hope I have also made clear that the statistical data of quantities of commodity and of prices used in the problem of the text have been taken merely to illustrate a statistical conception, and not to indicate what data should be selected to yield the most accurate demand curve.

Its graph is traced in Figure 4, and we see at a glance how the flexibility of prices of potatoes varies from point to point in the demand curve.

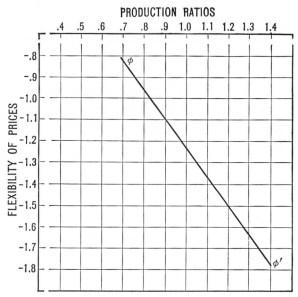

FIGURE 4.   The flexibility of the prices of potatoes.
$$\phi = 0.143 - 1.376(D/\bar{D}).$$

These results have been reached by starting with the typical equation of demand (8) in which quantity of commodity is taken as the independent variable. If the start had been made with the typical equation (11), in which price is the independent variable, the typical demand function in the ratio form would be

$$\frac{D}{\bar{D}} = B\left(\frac{p}{\bar{p}}\right)^{\beta} e^{\beta'(p/\bar{p})}. \qquad (20)$$

By following the same method as the one used in

fitting (15) to the data of observation, the above function (20) could be fitted to the same material. After the constants β and β' should have been determined concretely, we should have the law of variation of elasticity of demand, since, by hypothesis, the elasticity of demand is

$$\eta = \beta + \beta'\left(\frac{p}{\bar{p}}\right).$$

This concrete derivation of the law of variation of elasticity of demand would clear up the following perplexing statement by Marshall in his classic chapter, "The Elasticity of Wants": "The elasticity of demand is great for high prices, and great, or at least considerable, for medium prices; but it declines as the price falls; and gradually fades away if the fall goes so far that satiety level is reached. This rule appears to hold with regard to nearly all commodities and with regard to the demand of every class." [6] This statement is perplexing, because we have had no means of deriving empirical laws of demand and because it has been impossible to picture concretely what is meant by elasticity of demand being "great" or "considerable." We know when a coefficient of correlation is "great" or "considerable," but what is "considerable" or "great" elasticity of demand? Graphs of the values of η for various commodities, after the manner of the graph of ϕ in Figure 4, would answer the question.

The statistical methods that have just been described make possible the mastery of the problems to

[6] Marshall: *Principles of Economics*, 4th edition, p. 178.

which Cournot drew attention. He saw that many economic problems have different solutions according as the product of $pF(p)$ is increasing or decreasing for increasing values of p; and he recommended, as the first step toward a practical and rigorous solution of these problems, that commodities should be separated into two categories according as their current prices are above or below the value which makes a maximum of $pF(p)$. In the first section of this chapter we found that the distinction with which Cournot was concerned is the same as the modern distinction between commodities of elastic and of inelastic demand. Demand curves of type (20)

$$\frac{D}{\bar{D}} = B\left(\frac{p}{\bar{p}}\right)^{\beta} e^{\beta'(p/\bar{p})}$$

give summary descriptions of data within the limits in which p actually oscillates.[7] Moreover, since

$$\eta = \beta + \beta'\left(\frac{p}{\bar{p}}\right),$$

[7] Criticism is apt to degenerate into discussion of what might be the course of the curves beyond the limits of actual observation. It may not, therefore, be amiss to quote two authorities who would have been content to know what actually occurs within the limits of observation:

Cournot: "If we cease considering the question from an exclusively abstract standpoint, it will be instantly recognized how improbable it is that the function $pF(p)$ should pass through several intermediate maxima or minima inside of the limits between which the value of p can vary; and as it is unnecessary to consider maxima which fall beyond these limits, if any such exist, all problems are the same as if the function $pF(p)$ admitted only a single maximum. The essential question is always whether, for the extent of the limits of oscillation of p, the function $pF(p)$ is increasing or decreasing for increasing values of p." Bacon's translation of Cournot's *Researches*, p. 55.

this type, of course, likewise gives the law of the variation of elasticity with the variation of p.

Partial Elasticity of Demand and Partial Flexibility of Prices

The preceding sections of this chapter have presented the theory of demand as a function of a single variable and have described methods by which the theory may be given a concrete, statistical form. The remainder of the chapter will be devoted to a consideration of the more difficult problems of the theory and technique of demand when demand for any one commodity is regarded as a function of the prices of all commodities. To treat this more complex question there is need of a more ample notation, and to meet this requirement we shall take as our point of departure the notation of Walras.

Walras' symbols are as follows: The commodities produced in a unit of time are m in number and are represented by (A), (B), (C), $\cdot$ $\cdot$ $\cdot$. The factors of production fall into three classes: services of land, services of persons, and services of capital. The total number of services, for the unit of time, is assumed to be n, and these are designated as

Services of land (*terre*), (T), (T'), (T''), $\cdots$

Services of persons, (P), (P'), (P''), $\cdots$

Services of capital, (K), (K'), (K''), $\cdots$.

Marshall: "The general demand curve for a commodity cannot be drawn with confidence except in the immediate neighbourhood of the current price, until we are able to piece it together out of the fragmentary demand curves of different classes of society." *Principles*, 4th edition, p. 189.

If the commodity (A) is taken as a standard of value (*numéraire*) in terms of which the prices of commodities and services are expressed, the respective prices for the commodities may be represented as p_b, p_c, p_d, $\cdots$ and the respective prices for the services as $p_t \cdots$, $p_p \cdots$, $p_k \cdots$, $\cdots$. Since the prices of the $(m - 1)$ commodities are expressed in terms of the standard of value—commodity (A)—there are in Walras' system $(m - 1)$ demand functions, which he represents with these symbols:

$$
\left.
\begin{aligned}
D_b &= F_b(p_t,\ p_p,\ p_k,\ \cdots\ p_b,\ p_c,\ p_d,\ \cdots), \\
D_c &= F_c(p_t,\ p_p,\ p_k,\ \cdots\ p_b,\ p_c,\ p_d,\ \cdots), \\
D_d &= F_d(p_t,\ p_p,\ p_k,\ \cdots\ p_b,\ p_c,\ p_d,\ \cdots), \\
&\cdot\ \cdot\ \cdot\ \cdot\ \cdot\ \cdot\ \cdot\ \cdot\ \cdot\ \cdot\ \cdot\ \cdot\ \cdot
\end{aligned}
\right\} \quad (21)
$$

In these expressions the demand for any one commodity is regarded as a function not only of its own price but of the prices of all other commodities.

Walras' reasoning is limited to a static state. His quantities of commodities and prices are such as would prevail in his hypothetical construction, in a state of equilibrium, under a régime of perfect competition. To carry his reasoning into the sphere of economic realities, a method must be found for obtaining the concrete, complex functions of demand in a constantly changing society where perfect competition does not generally exist, and where equilibrium is incessantly perturbed.

In order to approach the real problem, let us recognize that all prices and all quantities of commodities are subjected to such forces as give to each of them an individual secular trend. Let us suppose that the secular trend of each price and of each commodity is determined statistically by fitting to the data, through the use of the method of least squares, a curve of type

$$y = a_0 + a_1 i + a_2 t^2 + a_3 t^3 + \cdots.$$

If the D's and p's are now taken as the actual quantities of commodities and the actual prices, their trend-values at a given time may be represented by putting a bar over these symbols, so that, for example, $\overline{D}_c$ will indicate the trend-value of the quantity of commodity (C) demanded at a time when the actual quantity of commodity demanded is D_c. Similarly $\overline{p}_c$ will indicate the trend-value of the price of (C) at the time the actual price is p_c. The new type of demand function will then be represented as

$$\frac{D_c}{\overline{D}_c} = F_c\left(\frac{p_t}{\overline{p}_t}, \frac{p_p}{\overline{p}_p}, \frac{p_k}{\overline{p}_k}, \cdots \frac{p_b}{\overline{p}_b}, \frac{p_c}{\overline{p}_c}, \frac{p_d}{\overline{p}_d}, \cdots \right). \quad (22)$$

This formula expresses the simple hypothesis that the trend-ratio of the quantity demanded is a function of the trend-ratios of all prices. While this hypothesis is simple it is the means of making the transition from a purely rational construction to a real situation. The introduction of the conception of a function of trend-ratios makes possible the statistical evaluation of the general demand function just as soon as its algebraic form is known.

When dealing with demand as a function of a single variable we reached appropriate typical demand curves by starting with the conceptions of elasticity of demand and flexibility of prices. Elasticity of demand, η, was defined as the ratio of the relative change in the quantity demanded to the relative change in price. Its formula is

$$\eta = \frac{dD}{D} \Big/ \frac{dp}{p} = \frac{p}{D} \cdot \frac{dD}{dp} \cdot \qquad (23)$$

Flexibility of price, ϕ, is the ratio of the relative change in the price to the relative change in the quantity demanded. Symbolically

$$\phi = \frac{dp}{p} \Big/ \frac{dD}{D} = \frac{D}{p} \cdot \frac{dp}{dD} \cdot \qquad (24)$$

If now demand, for example of commodity (C), is regarded as a function of all prices, the demand function is

$$D_c = F_c(p_t, \, p_p, \, p_k, \, \cdots \, p_b, \, p_c, \, p_d, \, \cdots). \qquad (25)$$

If price is regarded as a function of all quantities of commodities demanded, the price function is

$$p_c = f_c(D_t, \, D_p, \, D_k, \, \cdots \, D_b, \, D_c, \, D_d, \, \cdots). \qquad (26)$$

As a means of deriving concrete demand functions and concrete price functions, in place of (25) and (26), which are only abstract representations, the above procedure in case of a single variable suggests the wisdom of defining the conception of partial elasticity of demand and of partial flexibility of price.

If the demand function is in the form of (25), the partial elasticity of demand for commodity (C) with respect to p_t may be written, by following the analogy of (23),

$$\eta_{cp_t \cdot p_p p_k \cdots p_b p_c p_d \cdots} = \frac{p_t}{D_c} \cdot \frac{\partial D_c}{\partial p_t} \cdot \qquad (26a)$$

In this notation the primary subscripts of η are separated by a single dot from the secondary subscripts, and the whole symbol indicates the partial elasticity of demand for commodity (C), with respect to price p_t, when the demand for (C) is a function of $p_t, p_p, p_k,$ $\cdots p_b, p_c, p_d, \cdots$. In a similar manner the partial elasticity of demand for the commodity with respect to every other price may be indicated.

If the price function is in the form

$$p_c = f(D_t, D_p, D_k, \cdots D_b, D_c, D_d, \cdots),$$

the partial flexibility of price for commodity (C) with respect to D_t may be written, by following the analogy of (24),

$$\phi_{cD_t \cdot D_p D_k \cdots D_b D_c D_d \cdots} = \frac{D_t}{p_c} \cdot \frac{\partial p_c}{\partial D_t}. \qquad (27)$$

Here, again, the primary subscripts are separated by a single dot from the secondary subscripts, and the whole symbol indicates the partial flexibility of the price of commodity (C), with respect to D_t, when the price of (C) is regarded as a function of $D_t, D_p, D_k,$ $\cdots D_b, D_c, D_d, \cdots$.

Typical Demand Functions of More than One Variable

After developing general conceptions of partial elasticity of demand and partial flexibility of prices, we are confronted with the problem of determining the partial elasticities and partial flexibilities in particular cases. But a prerequisite to obtaining concrete results is the knowledge of appropriate types of demand functions and price functions. What steps may be taken toward finding these appropriate typical functions of demand and of price?

Obviously it is wise to go forward in the direction in which positive conclusions have already been attained. Progress in the treatment of elasticity of demand has been made (*a*) by using the method of trend-ratios in the preparation of the statistical data, and (*b*) by deriving appropriate demand curves from one of the hypotheses

$$\eta = \begin{cases} \beta, \text{ or} \\ \beta + \beta'p, \text{ or} \\ \beta + \beta'p + \beta''p^2. \end{cases}$$

The suggestions from this experience that occur with reference to the problem of the typical forms to be given to the representative demand function

$$D_c = F_c(p_t, p_p, p_k, \cdots p_b, p_c, p_d, \cdots)$$

are (*a*) to retain the method of trend-ratios in the preparation of the data, and (*b*) to derive increasingly complex typical functions that will give the partial elasticities with increasing accuracy. In case of the above representative demand function we know from equation (26*a*) that a representative partial elasticity of demand is

$$\eta_{cp_t \cdot p_p p_k \cdots p_b p_c p_d \cdots} = \frac{p_t}{D_c} \cdot \frac{\partial D_c}{\partial p_t}.$$

The increasingly complex demand functions, which give the partial elasticities with increasing accuracy, would obviously be obtained if functions could be found in which each partial elasticity of demand is given as a constant, or as varying in a linear function of the corresponding price, or as a quadratic function of the corresponding price. Supposing the functions discovered, we should then have, for the representative commodity (C), the partial elasticity of demand with respect to p_t in one of these three forms,

$$\eta_{cp_t \cdot p_p p_k \cdots p_b p_c p_d \cdots} = \frac{p_t}{D_c} \cdot \frac{\partial D_c}{\partial p_t}$$

$$= \begin{cases} \beta_{ct}, \text{ or} \\ \beta_{ct} + \beta'_{ct} p_t, \text{ or} \\ \beta_{ct} + \beta'_{ct} p_t + \beta''_{ct} p_t^2 \end{cases}. \quad (28)$$

In this notation the proper subscripts for the β's are the same as those of η, but abbreviated symbols have been used in order to avoid unwieldy formulas for the demand function in which, as we shall see, the β's are the parameters.

If, now, the first hypothesis in (28) is followed and the partial elasticities are assumed to be constant, the typical demand function for (C) is

$$D_c = Constant \ (p_t)^{\beta_{ct}}(p_p)^{\beta_{cp}}(p_k)^{\beta_{ck}}(\cdots)$$
$$\times (p_b)^{\beta_{cb}}(p_c)^{\beta_{cc}}(p_d)^{\beta_{cd}}(\cdots). \quad (29)$$

If the second hypothesis is followed, in which the partial elasticities are assumed to be simple linear functions of the corresponding prices, the typical demand function for (C) is

$$D_c = Constant \ (p_t)^{\beta_{ct}}(p_p)^{\beta_{cp}}(p_k)^{\beta_{ck}}(\cdots)$$
$$\times (p_b)^{\beta_{cb}}(p_c)^{\beta_{cc}}(p_d)^{\beta_{cd}}(\cdots)$$
$$\times e^{(\beta'_{ct} p_t + \beta'_{cp} p_p + \beta'_{ck} p_k + \cdots + \beta'_{cb} p_b + \beta'_{cc} p_c + \beta'_{cd} p_d + \cdots)}. \quad (30)$$

If the third hypothesis is followed, in which the partial elasticities are assumed to be quadratic functions of the corresponding prices, the typical demand function for (*C*) is

$$D_c = Constant \ (p_t)^{\beta_{ct}}(p_p)^{\beta_{cp}}(p_k)^{\beta_{ck}}(\cdots)$$

$$\times \ (p_b)^{\beta_{cb}}(p_c)^{\beta_{cc}}(p_d)^{\beta_{cd}}(\cdots)$$

$$\times \ e^{(\beta'_{ct}p_t+\beta'_{cp}p_p+\beta'_{ck}p_k+\cdots)+\frac{1}{2}(\beta''_{ct}p_t^2+\beta'_{cp}p_p^2+\beta''_{ck}p_k^2+\cdots)}. \quad (31)$$

In formulas (30) and (31) the symbol *e* is the base of natural logarithms.

That these three functions fulfil the conditions expected of them may be proved by showing that any one of the partial elasticities, for example,

$$\eta_{cp_t \cdot p_p p_k \cdots p_b p_c p_d \cdots},$$

is, in (29), a constant; in (30), a simple linear function of the corresponding price; in (31), a quadratic function of the corresponding price. To carry out the proof with regard to (29), take the logarithm of both sides of the equation; differentiate with respect to p_t; and then find the above representative partial elasticity. By following these directions we have

$$\log_e D_c = \log_e Constant + \beta_{ct} \log_e p_t + \beta_{cp} \log_e p_p$$

$$+ \cdots + \beta_{cb} \log_e p_b + \beta_{cc} \log_e p_c$$

$$+ \beta_{cd} \log_e p_d + \cdots.$$

Consequently,

$$\frac{1}{D_c} \cdot \frac{\partial D_c}{\partial p_t} = \frac{\beta_{ct}}{p_t},$$

whence

$$\eta_{cp_t \cdot p_p p_k \cdots p_b p_c p_d \cdots} = \frac{p_t}{D_c} \cdot \frac{\partial D_c}{\partial p_t} = \beta_{ct}.$$

By following the same directions with regard to (30), we have

$$\log_e D_c = \log_e \text{Constant} + \beta_{ct} \log_e p_t + \beta_{cp} \log_e p_p$$
$$+ \cdots + (\beta'_{ct} p_t + \beta'_{cp} p_p + \cdots).$$

Consequently,

$$\frac{1}{D_c} \cdot \frac{\partial D_c}{\partial p_t} = \frac{\beta_{ct}}{p_t} + \beta'_{ct},$$

whence

$$\eta_{cp_t \cdot p_p p_k \cdots p_b p_c p_d \cdots} = \frac{p_t}{D_c} \cdot \frac{\partial D_c}{\partial p_t} = \beta_{ct} + \beta'_{ct} p_t.$$

In a similar manner, proof may be given that, by following the same directions as in the preceding cases, equation (31) yields as the value of a representative partial elasticity

$$\eta_{cp_t \cdot p_p p_k \cdots p_b p_c p_d \cdots} = \frac{p_t}{D_c} \cdot \frac{\partial D_c}{\partial p_t} = \beta_{ct} + \beta'_{ct} p_t + \beta''_{ct} p_t^2.$$

Equations (29), (30), (31) are typical equations of demand, appropriate not only for connecting demand with prices but for supplying the derivative laws of the variation of partial elasticities of demand. If it is desired to regard price as the dependent variable, to take quantities of commodities demanded as the independent variables, and to arrive at laws of the variation of partial flexibilities of prices, the start would be made with the general price function

$$p_c = f_c(D_t, D_p, D_k, \cdots D_b, D_c, D_d, \cdots).$$

Partial flexibilities of prices could then be obtained with increasing accuracy if functions could be found in which the partial flexibilities are constants, or vary in simple linear functions of corresponding quantities of commodities demanded, or vary as quadratic functions of the corresponding quantities of commodities demanded. Supposing these price functions to be known, we should have for a representative commodity (C) the partial flexibility of price p_c with respect to D_t,

$$\phi_{cD_t \cdot D_p D_k \cdots D_b D_c D_d \cdots} = \frac{D_t}{p_c} \cdot \frac{\partial p_c}{\partial D_t}$$

$$= \begin{cases} \alpha_{ct}, \text{ or} \\ \alpha_{ct} + \alpha'_{ct} D_t, \text{ or} \\ \alpha_{ct} + \alpha'_{ct} D_t + \alpha''_{ct} D_t^2 \end{cases}. \quad (32)$$

If the first hypothesis is adopted, the typical price function is

$$p_c = Constant \ (D_t)^{\alpha_{ct}} (D_p)^{\alpha_{cp}} (D_k)^{\alpha_{ck}} (\cdots)$$
$$\times (D_b)^{\alpha_{cb}} (D_c)^{\alpha_{cc}} (D_d)^{\alpha_{cd}} (\cdots). \quad (33)$$

The second hypothesis yields as the typical price function

$$p_c = Constant \ (D_t)^{\alpha_{ct}} (D_p)^{\alpha_{cp}} (\cdots) (D_b)^{\alpha_{cb}} (D_c)^{\alpha_{cc}} (\cdots)$$
$$\times e^{\alpha'_{ct} D_t + \alpha'_{cp} D_p + \cdots}. \quad (34)$$

The third hypothesis gives

$$p_c = Constant \ (D_t)^{\alpha_{ct}} (D_p)^{\alpha_{cp}} (D_k)^{\alpha_{ck}} (\cdots)$$
$$\times (D_b)^{\alpha_{cb}} (D_c)^{\alpha_{cc}} (D_d)^{\alpha_{cd}} (\cdots)$$
$$\times e^{(\alpha'_{ct} D_t + \alpha'_{cp} D_p + \alpha'_{ck} D_k + \cdots) + \frac{1}{2}(\alpha''_{ct} D_t^2 + \alpha''_{cp} D_p^2 + \alpha''_{ck} D_k^2 + \cdots)}. \quad (35)$$

Statistical Derivation of Typical Demand Functions of more than One Variable

With the typical demand functions (29), (30), (31) and the typical price functions (33), (34), (35) before us, the next step is to fit the functions to the statistical observations. The observations themselves, however, refer to a constantly changing society: all of the variables that enter into the demand functions and price functions are themselves functions of time; and these typical functions must be adjusted so as to bring out the interrelations of prices and quantities of commodities not only at a particular time, but throughout a flow of time. To meet this need the device of trend-ratios, which was explained in detail in an earlier section of this chapter, is as applicable to functions of many variables as to functions of a single variable.

Repeating the notation used in an earlier section of this chapter, where symbols with bars placed over them refer to the trends of the variables, we may indicate the transformation which demand functions (29) and (30) undergo when trend-ratios are introduced. Demand function (29) becomes

$$\frac{D_c}{\overline{D}_c} = Constant \left(\frac{p_t}{\overline{p}_t}\right)^{\beta_{ct}} \left(\frac{p_p}{\overline{p}_p}\right)^{\beta_{cp}} \left(\frac{p_k}{\overline{p}_k}\right)^{\beta_{ck}} \left(\cdots\right)$$
$$\times \left(\frac{p_b}{\overline{p}_b}\right)^{\beta_{cb}} \left(\frac{p_c}{\overline{p}_c}\right)^{\beta_{cc}} \left(\frac{p_d}{\overline{p}_d}\right)^{\beta_{cd}} \left(\cdots\right), \quad (36)$$

or, in the logarithmic form,

$$\log\left(\frac{D_c}{\overline{D}_c}\right) = \log Constant + \beta_{ct} \log\left(\frac{p_t}{\overline{p}_t}\right)$$
$$+ \beta_{cp} \log\left(\frac{p_p}{\overline{p}_p}\right) + \cdots + \beta_{cb} \log\left(\frac{p_b}{\overline{p}_b}\right)$$
$$+ \beta_{cc} \log\left(\frac{p_c}{\overline{p}_c}\right) + \cdots. \quad (37)$$

Demand function (30) becomes

$$\frac{D_c}{\overline{D}_c} = Constant \left(\frac{p_t}{\overline{p}_t}\right)^{\beta_{ct}} \left(\frac{p_p}{\overline{p}_p}\right)^{\beta_{cp}} \left(\cdots\right)$$

$$\times \left(\frac{p_b}{\overline{p}_b}\right)^{\beta_{cb}} \left(\frac{p_c}{\overline{p}_c}\right)^{\beta_{cc}} \left(\cdots\right) e^{\beta'_{ct}\left(\frac{p_t}{\overline{p}_t}\right)+\beta'_{cp}\left(\frac{p_p}{\overline{p}_p}\right)+\cdots}, \quad (38)$$

or, in the logarithmic form,

$$\log\left(\frac{D_c}{\overline{D}_c}\right) = \log Constant + \beta_{ct} \log\left(\frac{p_t}{\overline{p}_t}\right)$$

$$+ \beta_{cp} \log\left(\frac{p_p}{\overline{p}_p}\right) + \beta_{ck} \log\left(\frac{p_k}{\overline{p}_k}\right)$$

$$+ \cdots + \left[\beta'_{ct}\left(\frac{p_t}{\overline{p}_t}\right) + \beta'_{cp}\left(\frac{p_p}{\overline{p}_p}\right)\right.$$

$$\left. + \beta'_{ck}\left(\frac{p_k}{\overline{p}_k}\right) + \cdots \right] \log e. \quad (39)$$

Equations (37) and (39) are linear functions of the β's, and hence the β's and the constants of integration may be directly ascertained by fitting these functions to the observations, either by the method of least squares or by the method which has become familiar in the theory of partial correlation. With the β's and the constants of integration empirically determined, we have the complex demand functions not only in concrete forms, but in such forms as give the partial elasticities of demand either as constants or as simple linear functions of the corresponding prices. If (37) is fitted to the data, a representative partial elasticity of demand is

$$\eta_{cp_t \cdot p_p p_k \cdots p_b p_c p_d \cdots} = \beta_{ct}.$$

If (39) is used, a representative partial elasticity of

demand, described as a simple linear function of the corresponding price, is

$$\eta_{cp_t \cdot p_p p_k \cdots p_b p_c p_d \cdots} = \beta_{ct} + \beta'_{ct} \left(\frac{p_t}{\bar{p}_t} \right).$$

Reasoning similar to the above with regard to the demand functions (29) and (30) and the adjusted trend-ratio forms (37) and (39) will hold with regard to the price functions (33) and (34) and the corresponding adjusted trend-ratio forms. These two types of demand functions and two types of price functions will probably suffice for most practical purposes, but if still more complex forms are required, resort may be had to types (31) and (35).

The prices and quantities of commodities to be used as raw data will be determined by the problem in hand: they may be of as many individual commodities as desired; or they may be of representative commodities of various categories; or they may be price index-numbers and corresponding quantity index-numbers of whole classes of commodities.

CHAPTER IV

THE LAW OF SUPPLY

"That fundamental symmetry of the general relations in which demand and supply stand to value, which coexists with striking differences in the details of those relations."

ALFRED MARSHALL

The fundamental symmetry with which demand and supply co-operate in the determination of price suggests the possibility, and indicates the desirability, that the typical functions descriptive of supply may be of the same general forms as those which have been found useful when dealing with demand. In the development of this chapter we shall see that, in fact, the actual practice of business and the exigences of economic theory concur in leading to the conclusion that the same typical functions reproduce the essential characteristics of both demand and supply.

Elasticity of Supply and Expansiveness of Supply Price

In the foregoing chapter we have seen that, if the demand for the representative commodity (C) is indicated as

$$D_c = F_c(p_c),$$

where D_c is the quantity of the commodity demanded at price p_c per unit of commodity, then elasticity of demand and flexibility of price may be expressed,

65

respectively, as

$$\eta_D = \frac{dD_c}{D_c} \bigg/ \frac{dp_c}{p_c} = \frac{p_c}{D_c} \cdot \frac{dD_c}{dp_c},$$

$$\phi_D = \frac{dp_c}{p_c} \bigg/ \frac{dD_c}{D_c} = \frac{D_c}{p_c} \cdot \frac{dp_c}{dD_c}.$$

These conceptions in the theory of demand are paralleled in the theory of supply with corresponding notions of elasticity of supply and of expansiveness of the supply price. Elasticity of supply is the ratio of the relative change of the quantity supplied to the relative change in the supply price. If S_c is adopted to indicate the quantity of commodity (C) supplied at price p_c and η_S is used to represent the elasticity of supply, the above definition becomes

$$\eta_S = \frac{dS_c}{S_c} \bigg/ \frac{dp_c}{p_c} = \frac{p_c}{S_c} \cdot \frac{dS_c}{dp_c}. \tag{40}$$

Expansiveness of supply price is the ratio of the relative change in supply price to the corresponding relative change in quantity of commodity supplied. If ϕ_S is used as the symbol for expansiveness of supply price, the above definition becomes

$$\phi_S = \frac{dp_c}{p_c} \bigg/ \frac{dS_c}{S_c} = \frac{S_c}{p_c} \cdot \frac{dp_c}{dS_c}. \tag{41}$$

Typical Supply Functions of One Variable

Elasticity of supply and expansiveness of supply price are conceptions that enter into the exact solution of many economic problems, and for this reason it is desirable to describe laws of supply by typical functions in which the characteristics of these two conceptions are revealed through the parameters of the functions. By following the method employed in the preceding chapter on "The Law of Demand," we may find typical functions of supply in which elasticity of supply is described as a constant, or as a simple linear function of the supply price, or as a quadratic function of the supply price. Increasingly complex supply functions are obtained by integrating the differential equations

$$\eta s = \begin{cases} \gamma_c, \text{ or} \\ \gamma_c + \gamma_c' p_c, \text{ or} \\ \gamma_c + \gamma_c' p_c + \gamma_c'' p_c^2. \end{cases}$$

If the elasticity of supply is assumed to be a constant and, in case of the representative commodity (C), equal to γ_c, we have

$$\eta s = \frac{dS_c}{S_c} \bigg/ \frac{dp_c}{p_c} = \gamma_c,$$

or

$$\frac{dS_c}{S_c} = \gamma_c \frac{dp_c}{p_c}.$$

Integrating, we get

$$\log_e S_c = \gamma_c \log_e p_c + \Gamma.$$

Or, passing from logarithms to absolute numbers, we have

$$S_c = \Gamma p_c^{\gamma_c}. \tag{42}$$

In this formula Γ is the constant of integration to be determined from the observations.

If the elasticity of supply is assumed to be a simple linear function of the supply price, the differential equation is

$$\eta s = \frac{dS_c}{S} \bigg/ \frac{dp_c}{p_c} = \gamma_c + \gamma_c' p_c,$$

which, when integrated, yields the typical supply function

$$S_c = \Gamma p_c^{\gamma_c} e^{\gamma_c' p_c}. \tag{43}$$

If the elasticity of supply is regarded as a quadratic function of the price,

$$\eta s = \frac{dS_c}{S_c} \Big/ \frac{dp_c}{p_c} = \gamma_c + \gamma_c' p_c + \gamma_c'' p_c^2$$

and the typical supply function is

$$S_c = \Gamma p_c^{\gamma_c} e^{\gamma_c' p_c + \frac{1}{2}\gamma_c'' p_c^2}. \tag{44}$$

These typical supply functions have been obtained by taking supply price as the independent variable and starting with three simple assumptions as to the character of elasticity of supply. If quantity of commodity is taken as the independent variable, we may derive corresponding typical functions by making similar assumptions as to the variation of expansiveness of supply price. We may put for the representative commodity (C)

$$\phi s = \frac{dp_c}{p_c} \Big/ \frac{dS_c}{S_c} = \begin{cases} \delta_c, \text{ or} \\ \delta_c + \delta_c' S_c, \text{ or} \\ \delta_c + \delta_c' S_c + \delta_c'' S_c^2. \end{cases}$$

By integrating these equations we obtain the typical supply functions

$$\left. \begin{array}{l} p_c = \Delta S_c^{\delta_c} \\ p_c = \Delta S_c^{\delta_c} e^{\delta_c' S_c} \\ p_c = \Delta S_c^{\delta_c} e^{\delta_c' S_c + \frac{1}{2}\delta_c'' S_c^2} \end{array} \right\} \tag{45}$$

In these equations the Δ's are constants of integration and e is the base of natural logarithms.

Statistical Derivation of Typical Supply Functions of One Variable

The typical supply functions which have just been deduced may be fitted to the observations in precisely the same manner as were the corresponding formulas referring to demand. As an illustration of that manner, the steps in fitting supply function (43) may be indicated. After the secular trends of prices and quantities of commodities have been computed by fitting to the representative data equations of type

$$y = a_0 + a_1t + a_2t^2 + a_3t^3 + \cdots,$$

the trend-ratios of the prices and quantities of commodities are calculated, and these trend-ratios constitute the raw data to which the typical functions are fitted. The typical functions are then transformed so as to show the trend-ratios, respectively, as the independent and dependent variables. For instance, supply function (43) is transformed into

$$\frac{S_c}{\bar{S}_c} = \Gamma \left(\frac{p_c}{\bar{p}_c} \right)^{\gamma_c} e^{\gamma_c'(p_c/\bar{p}_c)}, \tag{46}$$

where the symbols with bars placed over them are the trend-values of the variables. If, now, logarithms are taken of both sides of (46), we get

$$\log \left(\frac{S_c}{\bar{S}_c} \right) = \log \Gamma + \gamma_c \log \left(\frac{p_c}{\bar{p}_c} \right) + \gamma_c' \left(\frac{p_c}{\bar{p}_c} \right) \log e, \tag{47}$$

which may easily be fitted to the trend-ratio observations by the method of least squares. The statistical procedure is illustrated in detail in the chapter on "The Law of Demand."

Partial Elasticity of Supply and Partial Expansiveness of Supply Price

Thus far supply functions of a single variable have been derived which correspond, point for point, with demand functions of a single variable. This parallel treatment of supply and demand may be extended to functions of many variables. Corresponding to the conception of partial elasticity of demand, which led to the derivation of general demand functions of more than one variable, we may define the conception partial elasticity of supply, which will lead to general supply functions of more than one variable. In case of demand, we have found that, if the demand for representative commodity (C) is

$$D_c = F_c(p_t, \ p_p, \ p_k, \ \cdots \ p_b, \ p_c, \ p_d, \ \cdots),$$

the partial elasticity of demand for (C) with respect to a given price, for example, p_t, is

$$_D\eta_{cp_t \cdot p_p p_k \cdots p_b p_c p_d \cdots} = \frac{p_t}{D_c} \cdot \frac{\partial D_c}{\partial p_t}. \tag{48}$$

If, now, the law of supply of a representative service (T) is indicated by

$$S_t = F_t(p_t, \ p_p, \ p_k, \ \cdots \ p_b, \ p_c, \ p_d, \ \cdots), \tag{49}$$

the partial elasticity of supply with respect to a representative price, for example, p_c, may be defined as

$$_S\eta_{tp_c \cdot p_t p_p p_k \cdots p_b p_d \cdots} = \frac{p_c}{S_t} \cdot \frac{\partial S_t}{\partial p_c}. \tag{50}$$

In this notation the primary subscripts of η are separated by a single dot from the secondary subscripts, and the whole symbol indicates the partial elasticity of supply of service (T), with respect to price p_c, when the supply of (T) is a function of p_t, p_p, p_k, $\cdots$ p_b, p_c, p_d, $\cdots$. In a similar manner the partial elasticity of supply of the service (T) with respect to every other price may be indicated.

Partial elasticity of supply is defined by starting with supply as a function of all prices. Quite obviously, if the start is made with price as a function of all quantities of commodities supplied, for example,

$$p_t = f_t(S_t, S_p, S_k, \cdots S_b, S_c, S_d, \cdots), \qquad (51)$$

partial expansiveness of the supply price p_t with respect to S_c may be represented by

$$s\phi_{tS_c \cdot S_t S_p S_k \cdots S_b S_d \cdots} = \frac{S_c}{p_c} \cdot \frac{\partial p_t}{\partial S_c}. \qquad (52)$$

Typical Supply Functions of More than One Variable

In the foregoing chapter on "The Law of Demand," three types of general demand functions were found which give the partial elasticities of demand, respectively, as constants (29), simple linear functions of corresponding prices (30), and quadratic functions of corresponding prices (31). By following exactly the same method by which these results were reached in case of demand, similar corresponding results may be reached for supply.

Let us suppose that the proper method has been followed and the appropriate functions have been discovered: we should then have, for a representative service, (T), the partial elasticities of supply with respect to a representative price p_c, in these three forms

$$s\eta_{tp_c \cdot p_t p_p p_k \cdots p_b p_d \cdots} = \frac{p_c}{S_t} \cdot \frac{\partial S_t}{\partial p_c}$$

$$= \begin{cases} \gamma_{tc}, \text{ or} \\ \gamma_{tc} + \gamma'_{tc} p_c, \text{ or} \\ \gamma_{tc} + \gamma'_{tc} p_c + \gamma''_{tc} p_c^2 \end{cases}. \quad (53)$$

In this notation the proper subscripts of the γ's are the same as those for η, but the abbreviated symbols have been used in order to avoid unwieldy formulas for the supply functions in which, as we shall see, the γ's are parameters.

If, now, the first hypothesis in (53) is followed and the partial elasticities of supply are assumed to be constant, the typical supply function for the service (T) is

$$S_t = Constant\ (p_t)^{\gamma_{tt}} (p_p)^{\gamma_{tp}} (p_k)^{\gamma_{tk}} (\cdots)$$
$$\times (p_b)^{\gamma_{tb}} (p_c)^{\gamma_{tc}} (p_d)^{\gamma_{td}} (\cdots). \quad (54)$$

If the second hypothesis is followed, in which the partial elasticities of supply are assumed to be simple linear functions of the corresponding prices, the typical supply function for the service (T) is

$$S_t = Constant\ (p_t)^{\gamma_{tt}} (p_p)^{\gamma_{tp}} (\cdots)$$
$$\times (p_b)^{\gamma_{tb}} (p_c)^{\gamma_{tc}} (\cdots) e^{\gamma'_{tt} p_t + \gamma'_{tp} p_p + \cdots}. \quad (55)$$

If the third hypothesis is followed, in which the partial elasticities are assumed to be quadratic functions of the corresponding prices, the typical supply function for (T) is

$$S_t = Constant\ (p_t)^{\gamma_{tt}} (p_p)^{\gamma_{tp}} (\cdots) (p_b)^{\gamma_{tb}} (p_c)^{\gamma_{tc}} (\cdots)$$
$$\times e^{(\gamma'_{tt} p_t + \gamma'_{tp} p_p + \cdots) + \frac{1}{2}(\gamma''_{tt} p_t^2 + \gamma''_{tp} p_p^2 + \cdots)}. \quad (56)$$

In formulas (55) and (56), the symbol e is the base of natural logarithms.

That these three functions fulfil the conditions expected of them may be proved by showing that any one of the partial elasticities of supply, for example,

$$s\eta_{tp_c \cdot p_t p_p p_k \cdots p_b p_d \cdots},$$

is, in case of (54), a constant; in (55), a linear function of the corresponding price; in (56), a quadratic function of the corresponding price. To carry out the proof with regard to (54), take logarithms of both sides of the equation; differentiate with respect to p_c; and then find the above representative partial elasticity of supply. By following these directions we have

$$\log_e S_t = \log_e Constant + \gamma_{tt} \log_e p_t + \gamma_{tp} \log_e p_p$$
$$+ \cdots + \gamma_{tb} \log_e p_b + \gamma_{tc} \log_e p_c + \cdots.$$

Consequently,

$$\frac{1}{S_t} \cdot \frac{\partial S_t}{\partial p_c} = \frac{\gamma_{tc}}{p_c};$$

whence,

$$s\eta_{tp_c \cdot p_t p_p p_k \cdots p_b p_d \cdots} = \frac{p_c}{S_t} \cdot \frac{\partial S_t}{\partial p_c} = \gamma_{tc}.$$

By following the same directions with regard to (55), we have

$$\log_e S_t = \log_e Constant + \gamma_{tt} \log_e p_t + \gamma_{tp} \log_e p_p$$
$$+ \cdots + (\gamma'_{tt} p_t + \gamma'_{tp} p_p + \cdots).$$

Consequently,

$$\frac{1}{S_t} \cdot \frac{\partial S_t}{\partial p_c} = \frac{\gamma_{tc}}{p_c} + \gamma'_{tc};$$

whence,

$$s\eta_{tp_c \cdot p_t p_p p_k \cdots p_b p_d \cdots} = \frac{p_c}{S_t} \cdot \frac{\partial S_t}{\partial p_c} = (\gamma_{tc} + \gamma'_{tc} p_c).$$

In a similar manner proof may be given that, by following the same directions as in the preceding cases, equation (56) yields as the value of the representative elasticity of supply

$$s\eta_{tp_c \cdot p_t p_p p_k \cdots p_b p_d \cdots} = \frac{p_c}{S_t} \cdot \frac{\partial S_t}{\partial p_c} = (\gamma_{tc} + \gamma'_{tc} p_c + \gamma''_{tc} p_c^2).$$

Equations (54), (55), and (56) are typical supply functions appropriate not only for connecting supply with prices, but for ascertaining the derivative laws of the variation of partial elasticities of supply. If it is desired to regard price as the dependent variable, to take quantities of commodities supplied as the independent variables, and to arrive at laws of variation of partial expansiveness of supply prices, the start would be made with the representative function

$$p_t = f(S_t, S_p, S_k, \cdots S_b, S_c, S_d, \cdots).$$

Partial expansiveness of supply prices could then be obtained with increasing accuracy if functions could be found in which the coefficients of partial expansiveness are constants, or vary in simple linear functions of corresponding quantities supplied, or vary as quadratic functions of those quantities. Supposing these functions known, we should have for a representative service (T), the partial expansiveness of p_t with respect to S_c,

$$s\phi_{tS_c \cdot S_t S_p S_k \cdots S_b S_d \cdots} = \frac{S_c}{p_t} \cdot \frac{\partial p_t}{\partial S_c}$$

$$= \begin{cases} \delta_{tc}, \text{ or} \\ \delta_{tc} + \delta'_{tc} S_c, \text{ or} \\ \delta_{tc} + \delta'_{tc} S_c + \delta''_{tc} S_c^2 \end{cases}. \quad (57)$$

If the first hypothesis is adopted, the typical function
is

$$p_t = Constant \; (S_t)^{\delta_{tt}}(S_p)^{\delta_{tp}}(S_k)^{\delta_{tk}}(\cdots)$$
$$\times \; (S_b)^{\delta_{tb}}(S_c)^{\delta_{tc}}(S_d)^{\delta_{td}}(\cdots). \quad (58)$$

The second hypothesis yields as the typical function

$$p_t = Constant \; (S_t)^{\delta_{tt}}(S_p)^{\delta_{tp}}(\cdots)(S_b)^{\delta_{tb}}(S_c)^{\delta_{tc}}(\cdots)$$
$$\times \; e^{(\delta'_{tt}S_t + \delta'_{tp}S_p + \cdots)}. \quad (59)$$

The third hypothesis leads to

$$p_t = Constant \; (S_t)^{\delta_{tt}}(S_p)^{\delta_{tp}}(\cdots)$$
$$\times \; e^{(\delta'_{tt}S_t + \delta'_{tp}S_p + \cdots) + \frac{1}{2}(\delta''_{tt}S_t^2 + \delta''_{tp}S_p^2 + \cdots)}. \quad (60)$$

Statistical Derivation of Typical Supply Functions of More than One Variable

To fit to the observations the typical functions
(54), (55), (56), (58), (59), (60), they are first transformed so that they relate to trend-ratios instead of
absolute quantities; these adjusted functions are then
put into logarithmic forms, which are fitted to the
trend-ratio observations by the method of least
squares. An illustration of the procedure may be
given by indicating the steps in case of (55). For
practical purposes, where all prices and all quantities
of commodities are in a state of flux, (55) becomes, by
substitution of trend-ratios for absolute quantities,

$$\frac{S_t}{\overline{S}_t} = Constant \left(\frac{p_t}{\overline{p}_t}\right)^{\gamma_{tt}} \left(\frac{p_p}{\overline{p}_p}\right)^{\gamma_{tp}} (\cdots)$$
$$\times \; e^{\left\{\gamma'_{tt}\left(\frac{p_t}{\overline{p}_t}\right) + \gamma'_{tp}\left(\frac{p_p}{\overline{p}_p}\right) + \cdots\right\}}. \quad (61)$$

This typical trend-ratio function is now put into the

logarithmic form

$$\log\left(\frac{S_t}{\overline{S}_t}\right) = \log\ Constant + \gamma_{tt}\log\left(\frac{p_t}{\overline{p}_t}\right)$$
$$+ \gamma_{tp}\log\left(\frac{p_p}{\overline{p}_p}\right) + \cdots + \left\{\gamma'_{tt}\left(\frac{p_t}{\overline{p}_t}\right)\right.$$
$$\left. + \gamma'_{tp}\left(\frac{p_p}{\overline{p}_p}\right) + \cdots\right\}\log e. \quad (62)$$

As (62) is a linear function of the γ's it may be easily fitted to the trend-ratio observations by the method of least squares.

Relative Cost of Production (κ) and Relative Efficiency of Organization (ω)

In consequence of the ceaseless changes in the conditions of business, a representative entrepreneur is constantly asking, and constantly answering, the question whether he shall increase or diminish the quantity of his physical output. His decisions are made from the point of view of the probable movement of demand, which is beyond his control, and from the point of view of the efficiency of his own organization, which he is capable of modifying. This latter phase of the business problem relates to supply, and the criterion upon which his decision turns should have a technical name.

The quantities that are compared by the entrepreneur are total cost and total physical output. If total physical output is regarded as the independent variable and total cost as the dependent variable, the proposed criterion may be called the coefficient of relative cost of production and may be represented by κ. Relative cost of production, κ, may then be defined as the ratio of the relative change of the total cost to the relative change in total production. If y equals the total cost of production, and x, the total quantity produced, the symbolic representation of relative cost of production is

$$\kappa = \frac{\Delta y}{y} \Big/ \frac{\Delta x}{x},$$

or, at the limit,

$$\kappa = \frac{x}{y} \cdot \frac{dy}{dx}. \quad \text{If } y = \phi(x), \quad \kappa = \frac{x\phi'(x)}{\phi(x)}.$$

This criterion gives the information desired by the entrepreneur. He wishes to know, if he increase his output, whether the relative increase in total cost will be greater than, equal to, or less than the relative increase in the output. That is to say, he wishes to know whether $\kappa \gtreqless 1$.

If total cost is regarded as the independent variable and total output as the dependent variable, the criterion may be called the coefficient of relative efficiency of organization, and be represented by the symbol ω. Relative efficiency of organization, ω, is then defined as the ratio of the relative change in total production to the relative change in total cost. Symbolically,

$$\omega = \frac{dx}{x} \Big/ \frac{dy}{y} = \frac{\phi(x)}{x\phi'(x)}.$$

The information desired by the entrepreneur is whether $\omega \gtreqless 1$.

These criteria, κ and ω, not only will facilitate the theoretical treatment of the laws of cost, but, in the next chapter, will be of critical importance in statistical studies of coefficients of production.

Laws of Relative Cost and Relative Return Contrasted with Laws of Cost and Laws of Return

A description in mathematical terms of laws of economic return was first given by Cournot.[1] Cournot shows that if $y = \phi(x)$ is the expression for total cost of production, then there are three types of laws of cost or return, according as $\phi''(x) \gtreqqless 0$. He avoided many difficulties by contenting himself with a mathematical definition of the laws without passing on to identify them by name as the law of diminishing return, the law of constant return, and the law of increasing return. Without using the customary unprecise designations, he amply made good his claim that the condition $\phi''(x) \gtreqqless 0$ is of great importance in the solution of the principal problems of economic science.[2] It would be conducive to clearness and accuracy if the Cournot criterion $\phi''(x)$ were regarded as the criterion of laws of cost or laws of return.

In the preceding section the coefficient of relative return, or of relative cost, was defined as

$$\kappa = \frac{x}{y} \cdot \frac{dy}{dx} = \frac{x\phi'(x)}{\phi(x)} \cdot$$

[1] Cournot: *Recherches sur les principes mathématiques de la théorie des richesses*, p. 66, §§ 29–30. He considers, in addition to the above three cases, a fourth, where $\phi(x)$ is a constant.

[2] Cournot: *Recherches*, p. 65: "Dans la suite de nos recherches, nous aurons rarement occasion de considérer directement la function $\phi(D)$ [the $\phi(x)$ of the text], mais seulement son coefficient différentiel $d\phi(D)/dD$ que nous désignerons par la characteristique $\phi'(D)$. Ce coefficient différentiel est une nouvelle fonction de D, dont la forme exerce la plus grande influence sur la solution des principaux problèmes de la science économique. La fonction $\phi'(D)$ est, selon la nature des forces productrices et des denrées produites, susceptible de croître ou de décroître quand D augmente."

According as $\kappa \gtreqless 1$ we have to do with the law of increasing relative cost, or of diminishing relative return; the law of constant relative cost, or of constant relative return; the law of decreasing relative cost, or of increasing relative return. Just as Cournot's criterion $\phi''(x)$ is the criterion of laws of cost or of return, so the coefficient κ may be regarded as the criterion of laws of relative cost or of relative return.

The difference between the two conceptions may be illustrated. Suppose, for example, it is required to show the difference between the law of diminishing return and the law of diminishing relative return. The two criteria are

$$\phi''(x) > 0, \tag{63}$$

$$\kappa > 1. \tag{64}$$

But, by definition,

$$\kappa = \frac{x\phi'(x)}{\phi(x)},$$

and, as a result of the inequality (64), the law of diminishing relative return gives the information that

$$\phi'(x) > \frac{\phi(x)}{x}. \tag{65}$$

That is to say, in stating the law of diminishing relative return we assume that the marginal cost of production is greater than the average cost of production.

The inequality in (65) may be written

$$x\phi'(x) > \phi(x). \tag{66}$$

This states the well-known proposition in economic theory that where the law of diminishing relative return prevails, the ordinate of the integral supply curve is greater than the corresponding ordinate of the total cost curve. Economic theory has also led to the conclusion that under these conditions the slope of the supply curve is greater than the slope of the cost curve. This means that

$$\frac{d}{dx}\{x\phi'(x)\} > \phi'(x). \tag{67}$$

That is,

$$[\phi'(x) + x\phi''(x)] > \phi'(x), \quad \text{or} \quad \phi''(x) > 0. \tag{68}$$

Here we reach a conclusion in case of diminishing return and diminishing relative return which, by similar reasoning with regard to constant relative return and to increasing relative return, may be proved to be general, namely, where a given condition of κ holds, so likewise does the corresponding condition with reference to $\phi''(x)$ hold. In this particular case, we started in (64) with $\kappa > 1$ and we reached, in (68), $\phi''(x) > 0$. Where the law of diminishing relative return exists, there likewise does the law of diminishing return exist. The latter conception is at least as broad as the former: we shall now proceed to show that it is broader.

Auspitz and Lieben have described how a total cost curve is made up of bits of individual expense curves. Following their method of exposition,[3] let us suppose that an individual producer has such a plant that he can produce, with moderate variations of outlay, a quantity of commodity ranging between m_1 and m_1'

[3] Auspitz und Lieben: *Untersuchungen über die Theorie des Preises*, p. 112, Fig. 27 a.

(see Figure 5), and let us assume, further, that the total cost of producing quantities between m_1 and m_1' is given by the respective ordinates of the curve c_1c_1', which, by hypothesis, is assumed to be, throughout its extent, convex to the axis of x. If $\phi_1(x)$ is put for the integral cost curve of this producer (1), the convexity of the curve requires that $\phi_1''(x) > 0$, and, consequently, that the business be subject to the law of diminishing return between the limits

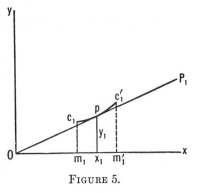

FIGURE 5.

$x = m_1$ and $x = m_1'$. Suppose, now, that the price of the commodity is given by the price line oP_1. At the price *tan* P_1ox, producer (1) could not afford to produce less nor more than ox_1, for which quantity the total cost would be y_1. But when ox_1 units of the commodity are produced we have

$$\frac{dy}{dx} = \frac{y_1}{x_1}.$$

For any point on the cost curve between c_1 and p, we have

$$\frac{dy}{dx} = \phi_1'(x) < \frac{y}{x},$$

and, consequently, by the criterion κ, the industry is subject between these limits to the law of increasing relative return. For any point on the cost curve between p and c_1', we have

$$\frac{dy}{dx} = \phi_1'(x) > \frac{y}{x},$$

and, consequently, by the criterion κ, the business between these limits is subject to the law of diminishing relative return.[4]

The result in this particular case of diminishing return is general: The criterion $\phi''(x)$ is more inclusive than the criterion κ: where κ occurs in a particular form the corresponding form of $\phi''(x)$ always occurs; but where $\phi''(x)$ exists in any particular form, the corresponding condition of κ may or may not be fulfilled.

Cost Curves and Supply Curves; Relative Cost Curves and Relative Supply Curves

The supply functions thus far described in this chapter are derivable immediately from the data of prices and quantities of commodities supplied. When the supply curves are known, it is possible to deduce from principles of economic theory the corresponding cost curves. There are, however, many cases where it is desirable to begin with cost data, to derive therefrom cost curves, and then to deduce, by means of principles of economic theory, the corresponding supply curves. If this need is to be met it is clearly desirable, in view of the critical importance of laws of cost in the solution of practical problems, to choose typical cost functions that shall reveal the nature either of $\phi''(x)$ or of κ.

[4] This point, as far as I am aware, was first made by Edgeworth. *Economic Journal*, June, 1899, p. 294.

We shall derive the cost functions and supply functions first by means of $\phi''(x)$. The simplest possible assumptions as to the nature of $\phi''(x)$ are summarized in (69):

$$\phi''(x) = \left\{ \begin{array}{l} m, \text{ or} \\ m + m'x, \text{ or} \\ m + m'x + m''x^2 \end{array} \right\} . \qquad (69)$$

If $\phi''(x) = m$, then $\phi'(x) = mx + \mu$, and the variation of marginal cost is described by a straight line. When the law of diminishing return dominates the industry, $\phi'(x) = mx + \mu$ is the equation to the supply curve. In that case, if p_s is put for the supply price per unit of commodity, the supply equation is $p_s = mx + \mu$. When the law of constant return regulates the industry, $m = 0$, $\phi'(x) = $ a constant, and the supply price is $p_s = \phi(x)/x$. When the law of increasing return prevails, the supply price [5] is likewise $p_s = \phi(x)/x$. More complex cost functions and corresponding supply functions could be deduced from the other assumptions in (69).

The criterion κ leads to other useful types of cost functions and supply functions. The simplest possible assumptions as to the nature of κ are summarized in (70):

$$\kappa = \left\{ \begin{array}{l} k, \text{ or} \\ k + k'x, \text{ or} \\ k + k'x + k''x^2 \end{array} \right\} . \qquad (70)$$

Suppose that $\kappa = k$, a constant. Since by definition

[5] Marshall: *Principles of Economics*, 4th edition, p. 539, note 1, Fig. 36.

the coefficient $\kappa = (x/y) \cdot (dy/dx)$, the hypothesis becomes

$$\frac{x}{y} \cdot \frac{dy}{dx} = k, \qquad \text{or} \qquad \frac{dy}{y} = k\frac{dx}{x}.$$

Integrating this last equation, we have

$$y = Constant\ x^k \equiv \phi(x), \qquad (71)$$

which is the law of the variation of total cost with the quantity of commodity that is produced.

The derivation of the equation to the supply curve from the equation to the cost curve will vary according as $\kappa \gtreqless 1$, that is, according as the business is subject to increasing, constant, or diminishing relative cost. When the industry is subject to increasing relative cost, κ is greater than unity; the supply price p_s is equal to the marginal cost of production, $\phi'(x)$; and the equation to the supply curve is

$$p_s = \phi'(x) = Constant\ kx^{k-1}. \qquad (72)$$

When the industry is subject to constant relative cost, $\kappa = 1$, and the supply price per unit of commodity is equal to the mean cost of production, that is,

$$p_s = \frac{\phi(x)}{x} = Constant\ x^{k-1} = Constant,$$

$$\text{since } k = 1. \quad (73)$$

When the industry is subject to decreasing relative cost, $\kappa < 1$, and the supply price per unit of commodity is equal to the mean cost of production, that is,

$$p_s = \frac{\phi(x)}{x} = Constant\ x^{k-1}. \qquad (74)$$

In the preceding discussion, laws of supply have been deduced from laws of cost, and the equations

(72), (73), (74) show that an expression of the type $y = Constant\ x^k$ is an appropriate form for the law of supply whatever may be the constant value of κ. It will, therefore, be allowable to take this type of function to describe the law of supply directly and then deduce from it the corresponding law of cost. This characteristic is valuable in treating supply and cost concretely: When it is impossible to find statistical data to serve as material for an empirical cost curve, it is sometimes [6] practicable to obtain directly from statistical data the curve of supply as a function of one variable from which, according to the above reasoning, the law of cost may be immediately deduced.

Just as the typical equation, $y = Constant\ x^k$, has been derived from the simplest hypothesis regarding the value of κ, so, by similar reasoning, more complex functions may be derived from other hypotheses in (70). If, for example, it be assumed that the variation of κ is linear, we have

$$\kappa = \frac{x}{y} \cdot \frac{dy}{dx} = k + k'x,$$

and the typical equation to the cost curve, from which the supply curve may be deduced, is

$$y = \phi(x) = Constant\ x^k e^{k'x}. \tag{75}$$

Partial Relative Efficiencies of Organization

There are three classes of general functions that appear in the theory of moving general equilibria: functions of demand, functions of supply, and pro-

[6] An instance is given in the following chapter under the section "A Moving Equilibrium of Supply and Demand."

duction functions. In the concrete, practical theory of moving equilibria these three classes of functions must be known not only in their algebraic mathematical forms, but in the numerical definiteness of their parameters. The studies of the foregoing and present chapters have met these desiderata for the demand functions and the supply functions. The means of arriving at a knowledge of the algebraic forms of the demand functions and supply functions was, in the former case, the theory of partial elasticity of demand; and in the latter case, the theory of partial elasticity of supply. The method of fitting the general algebraic functions to the statistical data was in both cases the method of trend-ratios.

Of these three classes of general functions there remains to be dealt with only the third, the production functions. We have to find appropriate algebraic forms of these functions and, then, to fit them to empirical data. The clue to the solution of the first problem is the theory of partial relative efficiency of organization.

The conception, relative efficiency of organization, which is symbolically represented by ω, we have already defined as the ratio of the relative change in total production to the relative change in total cost. If we suppose that Q_c represents the quantity of commodity (C) which is produced and we assume, as a first approximation, that the cost consists only of services of persons, which are represented in Walras' notation by (P_c), the relation between quantity produced and cost of services may be indicated by

$$Q_c = \Psi_c(P_c), \tag{76}$$

and the relative efficiency of organization, according to the above definition, would be

$$\omega = \frac{dQ_c}{Q_c} \Big/ \frac{dP_c}{P_c} = \frac{P_c}{Q_c} \cdot \frac{dQ_c}{dP_c}. \tag{77}$$

If, now, total cost is made up of services of land, services of persons, and services of capital, and the respective quantities of these are represented by T_c, P_c, K_c, $\cdots$, we have as the expression for the general production function

$$Q_c = \Psi_c(T_c, P_c, K_c, \cdots). \tag{78}$$

In treating this more complex function we are led, by analogy with the reasoning employed in the study of demand functions and supply functions, to the conception of partial efficiencies of organization, which may be symbolically indicated as follows:

$$\left. \begin{aligned} \omega_{ct \cdot pk \cdots} &= \frac{T_c}{Q_c} \cdot \frac{\partial Q_c}{\partial T_c} \\[2mm] \omega_{cp \cdot tk \cdots} &= \frac{P_c}{Q_c} \cdot \frac{\partial Q_c}{\partial P_c} \\[2mm] \omega_{ck \cdot tp \cdots} &= \frac{K_c}{Q_c} \cdot \frac{\partial Q_c}{\partial K_c} \end{aligned} \right\}. \tag{79}$$

The meaning of these coefficients is clear from their analogy with the coefficients of partial elasticity of demand and of partial elasticity of supply. For example, the first coefficient in (79) is the partial efficiency of organization with respect to the service (T_c) when the factors employed in the production of (C) are T_c, P_c, K_c, $\cdots$.

Typical Production Functions

One of the greatest difficulties in dealing with moving general equilibria is the problem of the determination of the coefficients of production. In the works both of Walras and of Pareto, these coefficients are purely hypothetical, and both economists assume, in their mathematical syntheses, that the coefficients are constants. To treat moving equilibria concretely and practically, typical functions must be found by means of which the coefficients may be derived from statistical data, and, moreover, the coefficients must be given in forms that approach reality with increasing accuracy. In the following chapter on "Moving Equilibria," the coefficients of production are shown to be functions of partial efficiencies of organization; in the remainder of this chapter, these coefficients of partial efficiency of organization are shown to be determinable as constants, or as simple linear functions of the corresponding factors of production, or as quadratic functions of the factors of production.

Typical functions of production may be derived in exactly the same way in which foregoing studies have derived typical functions of demand and typical functions of supply. Partial efficiencies of organization play the same rôle in production functions as partial elasticities of demand play in demand functions, and partial elasticities of supply, in supply functions. Suppose, for example, that the production functions for commodity (C) are to be determined and that the factors of production are (T_c), (P_c), (K_c), $\cdots$. Let a representative partial efficiency of organization be $\omega_{ct.pk}\ldots$. We may then impose upon the required functions the conditions that they shall give the partial efficiencies of organization as constants, or as linear functions of the factors, or as quadratic functions. These conditions, in case of the representative coefficient of partial efficiency of organization, are

$$\omega_{ct \cdot pk} \cdots = \begin{cases} \epsilon_{ct}, \text{ or} \\ \epsilon_{ct} + \epsilon'_{ct} T_c, \text{ or} \\ \epsilon_{ct} + \epsilon'_{ct} T_c + \epsilon''_{ct} T_c^2 \end{cases} \qquad (80)$$

If the partial efficiencies are to be constants, the first of the above conditions is followed, and we obtain as the typical production function

$$Q_c = Constant \ (T_c)^{\epsilon_{ct}} (P_c)^{\epsilon_{cp}} (K_c)^{\epsilon_{ck}} (\cdots). \qquad (81)$$

If the partial efficiencies are to be given as simple linear functions of the corresponding factors of production, the second of the above conditions is imposed, and the typical production function is

$$Q_c = Constant \ (T_c)^{\epsilon_{ct}} (P_c)^{\epsilon_{cp}} (K_c)^{\epsilon_{ck}} (\cdots)$$
$$\times e^{\epsilon'_{ct} T_c + \epsilon'_{cp} P_c + \epsilon'_{ck} K_c + \cdots}. \qquad (82)$$

If the partial efficiencies are to be given as quadratic functions of the factors of production, the third of the above conditions is chosen, and the typical production function is

$$Q_c = Constant \ (T_c)^{\epsilon_{ct}} (P_c)^{\epsilon_{cp}} (K_c)^{\epsilon_{ck}} (\cdots)$$
$$\times e^{(\epsilon'_{ct} T_c + \epsilon'_{cp} P_c + \epsilon'_{ck} K_c + \cdots) + \frac{1}{2}(\epsilon''_{ct} T_c^2 + \epsilon''_{cp} P_c^2 + \epsilon''_{ck} K_c^2 + \cdots)}. \qquad (83)$$

To fit (81), (82), (83) to statistical data, the variables, independent and dependent, are taken as trend-ratios and, in this transformed shape, are fitted to the observations by the method of least squares. When the trend-ratios are used as variables the three transformed functions are

$$\frac{Q_c}{\overline{Q}_c} = Constant \left(\frac{T_c}{\overline{T}_c}\right)^{\epsilon_{ct}} \left(\frac{P_c}{\overline{P}_c}\right)^{\epsilon_{cp}} \left(\frac{K_c}{\overline{K}_c}\right)^{\epsilon_{ck}} (\cdots), \qquad (84)$$

$$\frac{Q_c}{\overline{Q}_c} = Constant \left(\frac{T_c}{\overline{T}_c}\right)^{\epsilon_{ct}} \left(\frac{P_c}{\overline{P}_c}\right)^{\epsilon_{cp}} \left(\frac{K_c}{\overline{K}_c}\right)^{\epsilon_{ck}} (\cdots)$$
$$\times e^{\epsilon'_{ct}\left(\frac{T_c}{\overline{T}_c}\right) + \epsilon'_{cp}\left(\frac{P_c}{\overline{P}_c}\right) + \epsilon'_{ck}\left(\frac{K_c}{\overline{K}_c}\right) + \cdots}, \qquad (85)$$

$$\frac{Q_c}{\overline{Q}_c} = Constant \left(\frac{T_c}{\overline{T}_c}\right)^{\epsilon_{ct}} \left(\frac{P_c}{\overline{P}_c}\right)^{\epsilon_{cp}} \left(\frac{K_c}{\overline{K}_c}\right)^{\epsilon_{ck}} (\cdots)$$
$$\times e^{\left[\epsilon'_{ct}\left(\frac{T_c}{\overline{T}_c}\right) + \epsilon'_{cp}\left(\frac{P_c}{\overline{P}_c}\right) + \epsilon'_{ck}\left(\frac{K_c}{\overline{K}_c}\right) + \cdots\right] + \frac{1}{2}\left[\epsilon''_{ct}\left(\frac{T_c}{\overline{T}_c}\right)^2 + \epsilon''_{cp}\left(\frac{P_c}{\overline{P}_c}\right)^2 + \epsilon''_{ck}\left(\frac{K_c}{\overline{K}_c}\right)^2 + \cdots\right]}. \qquad (86)$$

As a preliminary to the use of the method of least squares in the evaluation of the ϵ's, logarithms are taken of both sides of equations (84), (85), (86). For example, (85) becomes

$$\log\left(\frac{Q_c}{\overline{Q}_c}\right) = \log Constant + \epsilon_{ct} \log\left(\frac{T_c}{\overline{T}_c}\right)$$
$$+ \epsilon_{cp} \log\left(\frac{P_c}{\overline{P}_c}\right) + \epsilon_{ck} \log\left(\frac{K_c}{\overline{K}_c}\right) + \cdots$$
$$+ \left[\epsilon'_{ct}\left(\frac{T_c}{\overline{T}_c}\right) + \epsilon'_{cp}\left(\frac{P_c}{\overline{P}_c}\right)\right.$$
$$\left. + \epsilon'_{ck}\left(\frac{K_c}{\overline{K}_c}\right) + \cdots\right] \log e, \qquad (87)$$

which is a linear function of the ϵ's and may, therefore, be easily fitted to the statistical data by the method of least squares.

Since the partial efficiencies may be determined empirically as constants, or as linear functions of the factors of production, or as quadratic functions of the factors; and since the coefficients of production, as we shall see in the next chapter, are known functions of the partial efficiencies, the problem of the values of the coefficients of production may be solved dynamically, concretely, practically.

CHAPTER V

MOVING EQUILIBRIA

"L'economia si presenta ora quale scienza delle leggi dell'equilibrio economico."

MAFFEO PANTALEONI

Synthetic Economics, in accord with the motto placed on the title page of this essay, seeks a "synthetic unification which transforms a plurality of discontinuous facts into a network of continuous relations." The discontinuous facts are prices and quantities of commodities and services. Our concrete demand functions, concrete supply functions, and concrete production functions express in mathematical form the relations between these prices, quantities of commodities, and quantities of services in terms of notions having critical significance in economic theory and practice. These notions are partial elasticities of demand, partial elasticities of supply, and partial relative efficiencies of organization. The present chapter weaves these concrete functions into a network of continuous relations describing the solidarity of exchange, production, capitalization, and distribution as a moving general equilibrium. We shall approach the general problem by beginning with particular equilibria.

A Moving Particular Equilibrium of Demand and Supply

According to Marshall,[1] "the general theory of the equilibrium of demand and supply is a fundamental idea running through the frames of all the various parts of the central problem of Distribution and Exchange." The general theory of equilibrium to which he refers is a theory of particular equilibrium, and throughout his work the treatment of particular equilibria is hypothetical, static, and limited to functions of one variable. Marshall recognized the impossibility of solving real problems by his method unless his hypothetical, static constructions could be replaced by concrete, dynamic functions, and sought to find a way in which the desiderata might be supplied. (*Principles*, 4th edit., pp. 188–191; 552–553.)

[1] Marshall: *Principles*, 4th edit., p. xi. The conception of this fundamental symmetry of demand and supply in the determination of price is usually attributed to Marshall, but in justice to Marshall we should recall that he himself gave the credit to Cournot: "Perhaps Jevons' antagonism to Ricardo and Mill would have been less if he had not himself fallen into the habit of speaking of relations which really exist only between demand price and value as though they held between utility and value; and if he had emphasized, as Cournot had done, and as the use of mathematical forms might have been expected to lead him to do, that fundamental symmetry of the general relations in which demand and supply stand to value, which coexists with striking difference in the details of those relations." (*Principles*, 4th edit., p. 569.)

It is all the more desirable to recall Marshall's just reference to Cournot because some of his critics seem to have overlooked his acknowledgment of Cournot's priority. Walras, in his criticism of Auspitz and Lieben, speaks of their curves of demand and supply as being no other than "courbes de demande et d'offre de Cournot et de Mangoldt dont se servent un certain nombre d'économistes anglais à la suite de M. Marshall de Cambridge." (*Éléments*, Quatrième édition, pp. 483–484.) Zawadzski (*Les Mathématiques appliquées à l'économie politique*, p. 301) credits to Cournot the method of presentation used by Marshall.

The studies we have just completed supply means of treating concretely a moving particular equilibrium of demand and supply. We know how to derive from statistics laws of demand and supply, and the methods are sufficiently general to avail not only when demand and supply are regarded as functions of one variable, but when both demand and supply are considered as functions of as many variables as the actual situation may require. The problem of a moving equilibrium of demand and supply when both demand and supply are functions of one variable alone may, therefore, be treated empirically by the methods with which we have become acquainted.

TABLE II

DATA FOR COMPUTING THE CURVES OF DEMAND AND SUPPLY. THE ANNUAL PRODUCTION OF POTATOES AND THEIR FARM PRICES, IN THE UNITED STATES

I Year	II December farm prices (cents per bushel)	III Production (millions of bushels)	IV Price trend-ratio	V Production trend-ratio	VI Price ratio of preceding year	VII Production ratio of current year
1900	43.1	211	0.794	0.988	....	....
1901	76.7	188	1.397	0.810	0.794	0.810
1902	47.1	285	0.850	1.144	1.397	1.144
1903	61.4	247	1.094	0.932	0.850	0.932
1904	45.3	333	0.798	1.191	1.094	1.191
1905	61.7	261	1.073	0.891	0.798	0.891
1906	51.1	308	0.877	1.011	1.073	1.011
1907	61.8	298	1.044	0.945	0.877	0.945
1908	70.6	279	1.179	0.860	1.044	0.860
1909	54.1	389	0.887	1.170	1.179	1.170
1910	55.7	349	0.898	1.029	0.887	1.029
1911	79.9	293	1.268	0.850	0.898	0.850
1912	50.5	421	0.788	1.207	1.268	1.207
1913	68.7	332	1.054	0.945	0.788	0.945
Mean	...	...	1.000	0.998	0.996	0.999

Suppose it is required to find the moving equilibrium of demand and supply in case of potatoes. Suppose, moreover, that both demand and supply are required as functions of one variable alone, namely, the quantity of potatoes put upon the market. Let the material in Table II, columns II and III, be the crude data. The problem, then, is to find from these data (*a*) the law of demand for potatoes as a function of the quantity of potatoes put upon the market; (b) the law of supply as a function of the same single variable; and (*c*) the moving equilibrium of demand and supply throughout the interval of fourteen years.

As the prices of potatoes and quantities of commodity put upon the market were both subject to secular changes throughout the interval under investigation, the secular trends of these two variables are ascertained by fitting to each of them a curve of type [2]

$$y = a_0 + a_1t + a_2t^2 + a_3t^3 + \cdots.$$

Columns IV and V of Table II give the ratios of the observations to their corresponding trends, and these two columns afford the data for the law of demand for potatoes. The data for the law of supply are given in columns VI and VII. In column VI the price trend-ratios given in column IV are advanced one year; the production trend-ratios in column VII are the same, year for year, as those given in column V. The correlation of the data for the law of demand for potatoes (columns IV and V) is $r = -0.95$; the correlation of the data

[2] In this particular problem only the first three terms of the above trend equation were used.

for the law of supply (columns VI and VII) is $r = + 0.80$.

In the chapter on "The Law of Supply" we have seen how the equation to the law of supply when it is deduced from the criterion $\phi''(x) = m$ is $p_s = mx + \mu$ {see equation (69)}; and when it is deduced from the criterion $\kappa = k$, it is of the type $p_s = Ax^k$ {see equation (72)}. Exactly corresponding types of equations may be used to describe the law of demand. A linear equation to the law of demand may be obtained in a manner corresponding to that in which, by use of Cournot's criterion $\phi''(x)$, the linear equation to supply was obtained from the equation to the cost curve. For example, let $F(x)$ be put for the money measure of the total utility of the commodity. Types of demand curves corresponding to the supply curves derived from $\phi''(x)$ will then be obtained by making the following hypotheses as to the value of $F''(x)$:

$$F''(x) = \begin{cases} a_1, \text{ or} \\ a_1 + b_1x, \text{ or} \\ a_1 + b_1x + c_1x^2 \end{cases} \qquad (88)$$

The demand equations deduced from (88) will then correspond with the supply equations derived from (89)

$$\phi''(x) = \begin{cases} a_2, \text{ or} \\ a_2 + b_2x, \text{ or} \\ a_2 + b_2x + c_2x^2 \end{cases} \qquad (89)$$

If, for example, the assumption is made that $F''(x) = a_1$ and $\phi''(x) = a_2$, the equation to the law of demand is

$p_d = a_1x + b_1$, and the equation to the law of supply is $p_s = a_2x + b_2$. Figure 6 shows these types of equations fitted to the data given, respectively, in columns IV and V, and in columns VI and VII of Table II.

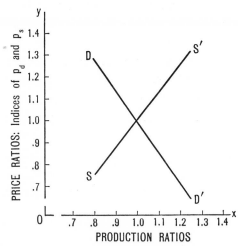

FIGURE 6. A moving equilibrium of demand and supply. Potatoes.

Demand: $p_d = -1.425x + 2.425$, origin $(0, 0)$;
Supply: $p_s = 1.222x - 0.222$, origin $(0, 0)$.

In addition to the technical advantage of having the equations to demand and supply in the simple linear form, there is the great theoretical gain of having the graphs of supply and demand pass exactly through the mean of the system of points in the scatter diagram. When the straight lines are fitted by the method of least squares, they must pass through the mean of the system of points. And when the production-ratios and price-ratios are deduced from trends of type

$$y = a_0 + a_1t + a_2t^2 + a_3t^3 + \cdots,$$

which are fitted to the data by the method of least squares, the means of these ratios are, within the limit of permissible error, equal to unity. In the particular case of the data referring to potatoes, Table II shows that this latter statement is true.

In consequence of the graphs of supply and demand passing through the point whose coördinates are (1.0, 1.0), the demand for the commodity and the supply of the commodity are in a moving equilibrium about the trends of prices and production. When, for instance, the supply price-ratio of a given year was unity, the production-ratio of the following year was unity; and when the production-ratio of that following year was unity, the demand price-ratio of the same year was unity.[3] These facts are illustrated in Figure 6.

[3] Repeatedly, in preceding chapters, we have noted the desirability of so choosing the types of the economic equations that their parameters shall reveal the nature of important economic coefficients, and we are therefore concerned to know whether either coefficient in these linear demand and supply functions has an economic significance. It may easily be proved that in case of the demand function,

$$p_d = a_1 x + b_1,$$

the quantity a_1 is the flexibility of demand prices at the point $x = 1.0$, $p_d = 1.0$; that is to say, a_1 is the coefficient of the flexibility of demand prices at the mean of the system of demand points. The proof is as follows:

By definition, the coefficient of flexibility of demand prices is

$$\phi_d = \frac{dp_d}{p_d} \Big/ \frac{dx}{x} = \frac{x}{p_d} \cdot \frac{dp_d}{dx}.$$

Since dp_d/dx is a_1, and since the straight line passes through the mean of the system of demand points, whose coordinates are $x = 1.0$, $p_d = 1.0$, we have $\phi_d = a_1$ at the mean of the system of demand points. In a similar manner the quantity a_2 in the supply equation $p_s = a_2 x + b_2$ may be proved to be the coefficient of the expansiveness of supply price (see Chapter III) at the point whose coordinates are $x = 1.0$, $p_s = 1.0$. A more general proof is given in footnote 14 of this chapter.

A second type of demand and supply functions is $y = Ax^\alpha$. In the chapter on "The Law of Demand" {Equation (7)}, we found that when the law of demand is of type $p_d = Ax^{\alpha_1}$, the exponent α_1 is the coefficient of flexibility of demand prices; and in the chapter on "The Law of Supply" {Equation (72)} we

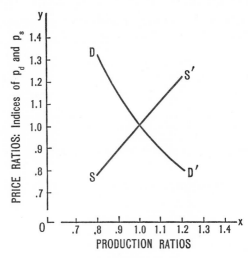

FIGURE 7. A moving equilibrium of demand and supply.
Potatoes.

Demand: $p_d = x^{-1.2310}$, origin $(0, 0)$;
Supply: $p_s = x^{1.0828}$, origin $(0, 0)$.

learned that when the law of supply is of type $p_s = A_2 x^{\alpha_2}$, the coefficient of relative cost of production, κ, is $\kappa = \alpha_2 + 1$. Before fitting these functions to the data we may effect a simplification by agreeing that when $x = 1.0$, $p_d = 1.0$, and $p_s = 1.0$. With this simplification, the demand function is $p_d = x^{\alpha_1}$, and the supply function is $p_s = x^{\alpha_2}$. If these functions are now taken in the forms

$$\log p_d = \alpha_1 \log x,$$
$$\log p_s = \alpha_2 \log x,$$

they may easily be fitted to the observations by the method of least squares. Figure 7 gives the result of the computation for potatoes and shows that here, again, there is a moving equilibrium of demand and supply about the secular trends of prices and production.

The preceding discussion of a moving equilibrium of demand and supply has gone forward with the use of only the simplest forms of demand curves and supply curves. No new principle would have been introduced if we had employed the more complex and more exact functions of one variable described in the foregoing two chapters.

Walrasian Equations

On June 10, 1909, there was placed on the wall of the *Académie* of Lausanne a bronze medallion portrait bearing this inscription:

À Léon Walras, né à Evreux en 1834, professeur à l'Académie et à l'Université de Lausanne qui, le premier, a établi les conditions générales de l'équilibre économique fondant ainsi "l'École de Lausanne." Pour honorer cinquante ans de travail désinteressé.

The chief claim of Léon Walras to scientific immortality does not lie in his having advanced, contemporaneously with Jevons and Menger, the marginal utility theory of value; nor in his elaborate plea for free trade; nor in his ingenious schemes of taxation and stable money, but, as indicated by the legend upon the Lausanne memorial tablet, in his having established for the first time the conditions of a general economic equilibrium.

Some fifteen years before the *Jubilé Walras* in 1909, Enrico Barone, himself an expert, expressed his admiration for the work of the Lausanne economist in these words: "Of theories of equilibrium we know no other up to the present time which is more general, more comprehensive, and more harmonious in all its parts than the very beautiful theory of Walras." [4]

Pareto, whose structure of pure economics rests upon a Walrasian foundation, was of the opinion that certain equations developed by his "venerated master" [5] "jouent dans l'étude de l'équilibre économique un rôle analogue à celui des équations de Lagrange dans l'étude de l'équilibre mécanique." [6] He has himself told how, at the first reading of the works of Walras, he had been repelled by the metaphysical conceptions which Walras employed in common with his contemporaries but which, according to Pareto, should have no place in experimental science. Under a subsequent inspiration from Pantaleoni, he reverted to the Walras inquiry and found there the golden conception of economic equilibrium. [7] That conception

[4] Barone: "Sul Trattamento di Quistioni Dinamiche." *Giornale degli Economisti* (1894), p. 407.

[5] " . . . mon vénéré maître, M. le Professeur Walras. L'étude de ses travaux m'a initié aux théories de l'économie mathématique et a été l'origine de mes propres recherches." *Jubilé Walras* (Lausanne, 1909), p. 55.

[6] Pareto: *Cours d'Économie Politique*, Vol. I, p. 25.

[7] "Avevo letto le opere del Walras, ed avevo lasciato l'oro per badare alla roccia sterile, cioè alle considerazioni metafisiche. Respinto da

dominates Pareto's work not only in economics, but also in sociology. In his view a necessary preliminary to sociological theory is an acquaintance with the economic theory of equilibrium.[8]

In its simplest form—the form that will be used later on in this chapter—the conditions of a general economic equilibrium as conceived by Walras are described by four groups of equations. If, as a methodological device, the fiction of a static state is resorted to, with the consequent corollary that no readjustment of expenditure on the part of consumers nor of the factors of production on the part of entrepreneurs will result in a gain, the conditions of the prevailing general equilibrium are described by the following groups of equations: (1) equations of demand for commodities; (2) equations of supply of productive services; (3) equations expressing the equality of the

queste, che mi parevano, e tuttavia mi paiono, assurde, non credevo che simili teorie potessero avere luogo nella scienza sperimentale. Ma dopo avere letto i *Principii* del Pantaleoni, si modificò in me questo concetto. Tornai a leggere le opere del Walras, e vi trovai l'oro, cioè il concetto dell'equilibrio economico; e così, posto sulla buona via, spero di avere trovato qualche teoria che si avvicini a quelle rigorosamente scientifiche che oramai dominano nelle scienze naturali, e che potrà servire sinchè altri ne trovi altre che meglio ancora abbiano tale carattere; a così si seguiterà sinchè progredirà la scienza." Vilfredo Pareto: "Economia Dimessa" (Bologna, 1912), p. 6. (*Estratto da La Libertà Economica,* Anno X, N. 17–18.)

[8] "Gli stati X_1, X_2, X_3, . . . sono analoghi a quelli che l'Economia pura considera per un sistema economico; e l'analogia è tanto grande che gli stati del sistema economico si possono considerare come casi particolari degli stati generali del sistema sociologico. . . . Questa materia non è facile, e credo quindi dovere aggiungere che stimo indispensabile che il lettore che desidera acquistare un concetto chiaro degli stati sociologici X_1, X_2, X_3 . . . , e dei modi possibili di determinarli, studi prima il fenomeno simile che si considera nelle teorie dell'Economia pura." Pareto: *Trattato di Sociologia Generale.* Seconda edizione, Vol. III, pp. 271, 272, 272 n.

quantities of services demanded to the quantity of services supplied; (4) equations expressing the equality of the prices of commodities with the respective costs of production.

Walras formulates his theory by means of the following symbols:

The commodities produced in a unit of time are m in number and are represented by (A), (B), (C) $\cdots$.

The factors of production fall into three classes: services of land, services of persons, and services of capital goods. The total number of the services, for the unit of time, is assumed to be n, and these are designated as

Services of land (*terre*), (T), (T'), (T''), $\cdots$

Services of persons, (P), (P'), (P''), $\cdots$

Services of capital, (K), (K'), (K''), $\cdots$.

If the commodity (A) be taken as a *numéraire* in terms of which the prices of commodities and services are expressed, the respective prices for the commodities may be represented as p_b, p_c, p_d, $\cdots$ and the respective prices of the services as $p_t \cdots$, $p_p \cdots$, $p_k \cdots$.

Since the prices of the $(m-1)$ commodities are expressed in terms of the *numéraire*—commodity (A)—there are $(m-1)$ demand functions, which Walras represents with these symbols:

$$\left.\begin{array}{l} D_b = F_b(p_t,\ p_p,\ p_k,\ \cdots\ p_b,\ p_c,\ p_d,\ \cdots), \\ D_c = F_c(p_t,\ p_p,\ p_k,\ \cdots\ p_b,\ p_c,\ p_d,\ \cdots), \\ D_d = F_d(p_t,\ p_p,\ p_k,\ \cdots\ p_b,\ p_c,\ p_d,\ \cdots), \\ \cdot\quad\cdot\quad\cdot\quad\cdot\quad\cdot\quad\cdot\quad\cdot\quad\cdot\quad\cdot\quad\cdot\quad\cdot \end{array}\right\} \quad (90)$$

In these expressions the demand for any commodity

is regarded as a function not only of its own price but of the prices of all commodities. These $(m - 1)$ demand functions constitute the first group of equations contributing to the description of a general equilibrium

Corresponding to these $(m - 1)$ equations of demand for commodities, there are n equations of supply of productive services. The n functions descriptive of supply are

$$\left.\begin{array}{l} S_t = F_t(p_t,\ p_p,\ p_k,\ \cdots\ p_b,\ p_c,\ p_d,\ \cdots), \\ S_p = F_p(p_t,\ p_p,\ p_k,\ \cdots\ p_b,\ p_c,\ p_d,\ \cdots), \\ S_k = F_k(p_t,\ p_p,\ p_k,\ \cdots\ p_b,\ p_c,\ p_d,\ \cdots), \\ \cdot\quad\cdot\quad\cdot\quad\cdot\quad\cdot\quad\cdot\quad\cdot\quad\cdot\quad\cdot\quad\cdot\quad\cdot\quad\cdot\quad\cdot \end{array}\right\} \quad (91)$$

These n equations of supply constitute the second group of conditions contributing toward the description of a general equilibrium.

As a means of deriving the next two groups of equations, Walras defines his understanding of coefficients of production. The coefficients of production (*coefficients de fabrication*) of a commodity (A) are the quantities of the services of the factors of production that enter into the manufacture of a unit of (A). Since the commodities produced are (A), (B), (C), $\cdots$ and the factors of production are (T), (P), (K), $\cdots$, the coefficients of production may be represented, respectively, by

$$a_t,\ a_p,\ a_k,\ \cdots$$
$$b_t,\ b_p,\ b_k,\ \cdots$$
$$c_t,\ c_p,\ c_k,\ \cdots$$
$$\cdot\quad\cdot\quad\cdot\quad\cdot\quad\cdot\quad\cdot$$

The coefficients of production are assumed by Walras to be constant in the static state.

We may now consider the third and fourth groups of equations determining the general equilibrium. Since there are n productive services, there are n equations expressing the equality of the quantities of services demanded to the quantities of the services supplied.

$$\left.\begin{aligned}
a_t D_a + b_t D_b + c_t D_c + d_t D_d + \cdots &= S_t, \\
a_p D_a + b_p D_b + c_p D_c + d_p D_d + \cdots &= S_p, \\
a_k D_a + b_k D_b + c_k D_c + d_k D_d + \cdots &= S_k,
\end{aligned}\right\} \quad (92)$$

These n equations of demand and supply are the third group of equations contributing toward the description of a general equilibrium.

In the general equilibrium of the static state the costs of production of the commodities must be equal to their prices, and since there are m commodities, there are m equations descriptive of the equality of cost and price. They are

$$\left.\begin{aligned}
a_t p_t + a_p p_p + a_k p_k + \cdots &= 1, \\
b_t p_t + b_p p_p + b_k p_k + \cdots &= p_b, \\
c_t p_t + c_p p_p + c_k p_k + \cdots &= p_c.
\end{aligned}\right\} \quad (93)$$

These m equations of cost and price constitute the fourth and last group of equations contributing to the description of a general equilibrium.

Theoretically the problem of a general equilibrium is now solved, because the number of the equations is equal to the number of the unknown quantities. There are $(2m + 2n - 1)$ unknown quantities, namely, the m quantities of the m commodities demanded; the

$(m - 1)$ prices of the m commodities in terms of one of them which is used as a standard of prices; the n quantities of the services that are supplied; and the n prices of the n services in terms of the standard of prices. To determine these unknown quantities there are $(2m + 2n - 1)$ equations, namely, the $(m - 1)$ equations of demand for the $(m - 1)$ commodities; the n equations of supply of the n services; the n equations expressing the equality of the quantities of the services demanded to the quantities of the services offered; and the m equations expressing the equality of the costs of production and the prices of the m commodities.

No mathematical economist, as far as I am aware, has ever attempted to pass from this or any similar presentation of a statical, hypothetical equilibrium to a realistic treatment of an actual, moving general equilibrium.[9]

[9] Representative views as to the impossibility of making the transition are those of Auspitz and Lieben, and of Edgeworth:

"Ebenso begnügen wir uns, den allgemeinen Formcharacter unserer Kurven zu ermitteln, und enthalten uns, eine Näherungsgleichung derselben zu geben, wie dies etwa mit Hilfe der Statistik für bestimmte Fälle versucht werden könnte. Die der Erfahrung entnommenen Angaben haben nämlich zwar einen historischen Wert, sind aber sonst schwer vergleichbar, da in verschiedenen Zeitmomenten nicht nur die Preisverhältnisse, sondern auch andere, vielleicht höchst wichtige Umstände sich geändert haben werden; solche Daten können also unserer Voraussetzungen nicht entsprechen. Überdies müsste eine Formel, die der Wirklichkeit genügen wollte, so unklar und verwickelt ausfallen, als es die Wirklichkeit selbst ist." Auspitz und Lieben: *Untersuchungen über die Theorie des Preises*, pp. xiv, xv.

Referring to the question of finding demand curves, "Es wird wohl nie möglich sein sich diese Kenntniss genau zu verschaffen." *Ibid.*, p. 373.

"M. Edgeworth croit bonnement qu'il est tout simplement oiseux de

The Premise of Free Competition: A Spurious Superfoetation

Walras entitled his work *"Éléments d'Économie Politique Pure"* and he took pains to explain his title by giving the following succinct definition of the pure science: *"L'économie politique pure* est essentiellement la théorie de la détermination des prix sous un régime hypothétique de libre concurrence absolue" (Quatrième édition, p. xi). The Walrasian equations which have just been presented constitute an essay in "pure political economy" in the Walrasian meaning of the terms: The equations of demand, the equations of supply, the coefficients of production are not deduced from reality but are hypothetical, and the equilibrium to which the mathematical conditions lead is an ideal, statical equilibrium which is attained on the supposition of *"un régime hypothétique de libre concurrence absolue."*

But what is *"la libre concurrence absolue"?* This same question has been asked and, I hope, answered in Chapter II of this Essay, in the section dealing with "The Premise of Free Competition." At least five hypotheses are subsumed under the expression "free competition" when "free competition" is made the fundamental premise of pure economics. It is assumed (*a*) that every economic factor seeks and obtains a maximum net income; (*b*) that there is but one

chercher à démontrer la voie suivant laquelle le système économique est amené à l'équilibre, et il trouve une confirmation de cette vue dans l'opinion émise par Jevons, à savoir que les problèmes relatifs à équilibre économique doivent être traités au point de vue statique et non pas dynamique." Ladislas Bortkévitch: "Léon Walras. Éléments d'économie politique pure, ou Théorie de la richesse sociale," *Revue d'économie politique* (Janvier–Février, 1890), p. 6.

price for commodities of the same quality in the same market; (*c*) that the influence of the product of any one producer upon the price per unit of the total product is negligible; (*d*) that the output of any one producer is negligible as compared with the total output; (*e*) that each producer regulates the amount of his output without regard to the effect of his act upon the conduct of his competitors. The discussion of Chapter II reached the conclusion that in actual economic life, which is in a state intermediate between perfect competition and perfect monopoly, the above hypothesis (*a*) is at best only approximately true; hypothesis (*b*) is frequently untrue; and hypotheses (*c*), (*d*), and (*e*), in many spheres, are never true. Pareto [10] has put the matter compactly: "La libre concurrence produit le maximum d'ophélimité; la libre concurrence règne dans nos sociétés: ce sont là deux propositions différentes. La première est très probablement vraie; la seconde est certainement fausse."

This categorical statement by Pareto seems to place the economist in a dilemma: If he wishes to continue the work of the pure economists, he must build upon a premise which is "certainement fausse," and, with the elaboration of his theoretical construction, he must depart further and further from reality; if he wishes to develop a positive science, consisting of summary descriptions of empirical fact making possible rational forecasting and control, he must modify or abandon the unreal premise of his predecessors. Supposing we decide in favor of the latter alternative, how shall we

[10] Pareto: *Cours d'économie politique.* Vol. II, p. 130, note (788)².

proceed to reformulate the fundamental premise of the science? We may state at once our conclusion: The fundamental premise of the science is "competition" in the original and real sense that every economic factor seeks a maximum net gain. This premise is implicit in Aristotle's treatment of chrematistics when he says "the art of money-getting seems to be chiefly conversant about trade, and its end—to be able to see where the greatest profit can be made." [11] All the other implications of "competition" listed above are illegitimate superfoetations of the mother term: They had their origin not in an inductive study of economic societies but in a supposed need for radical simplification as a condition of the use of the deductive method. Jevons [12] was responsible for putting upon "competition" the burden of the "law of indifference" {the above hypothesis (b)}, and Pareto [13] disclosed the methodological origin of the other spurious meanings {hypotheses (c), (d), (e)}, in his description of "free competition": "L'échangeur subit les prix du marché sans essayer de les modifier de propos délibéré. Ces prix sont modifiés effectivement par son offre et sa demande, mais c'est à son insu. *C'est ce qui caractérise l'état que nous appelons de libre concurrence.*" "En langage mathématique nous dirons que pour établir les conditions du maximum, on différentie en supposant les prix constants."

Time has given us an advantage over the founders

[11] Aristotle: *Politics.* Chapter IX. Bohn's Library edition, p. 22.

[12] W. S. Jevons: *Principles of Economics*, p. 60. "This law of indifference, in fact, is but another name for the principle of competition which underlies the whole mechanism of society."

[13] Pareto: *Cours d'économie politique*, Vol. I, p. 20 and 20 note (46)[1].

of the *École de Lausanne*. They felt compelled to work with hypothetical laws of demand, hypothetical laws of supply, and hypothetical coefficients of production while we, coming at a later date, are able in each case to work with real functions. The difference in the method of approach implies an essential difference in the whole conception of equilibria, and the newer conception rests upon no unreal premise. The *École de Lausanne*, starting with a fundamental premise which is "certainement fausse," were compelled to use, in their quest of a general equilibrium, abstract functions that were, by implication, compatible with this false fundamental premise: Their abstract functions of demand, abstract functions of supply, and abstract coefficients of production are such as would obtain *"sous un régime hypothétique de libre concurrence absolue."* The general equilibrium deduced by means of the unreal functions and the false premise not only lies under the imputation of being hypothetical and static, but cannot be made to resemble a real, moving equilibrium because the approach to reality would destroy the network of implications by means of which it exists. The situation is quite different when we start with real functions of demand, real functions of supply, and real coefficients of production. Since these functions are actually deduced from current statistics, they are not limited to "un régime hypothétique de libre concurrence absolue," but they hold in the actual, changing economic complex of competitive industries, partial monopolies, and complete monopolies. Since in the real economic complex a moving equilibrium in accord with these real functions is actually attained, the fundamental premise we are seeking must be a summary description of the condition under which the real functions lead to the real moving equilibrium. That condition is none other than the quest of maximum income on the part of every member of the economic society: it is "competition" in the fundamental meaning of the term, and there is no need to invoke an unreal premise of "libre concurrence absolue" nor to resort to an hypothetical static state in a stable equilibrium.

The Real Functions in a Moving General Equilibrium

The Walrasian equations suggest that three groups of real functions must be obtained from statistical data as a preliminary to the complete mathematical description of a moving general equilibrium. The three groups are real functions of demand, real functions of supply, and real coefficients of production. The methods of deriving the first and second groups were given, respectively, in the chapter on "The Law of Demand" and the chapter on "The Law of Supply." In the next section the means of deriving the coefficients of production will be developed, and we may anticipate the discussion as far as to say the coefficients of production will be shown to be dependent upon the production functions, the derivation of which we have already considered. These three groups of real functions may, in each case, take three typical forms which have parameters describing fundamental conceptions in economic theory and which reproduce the statistical data with increasing accuracy. As we found in our chapter on "The Law of Demand," the three typical functions of demand for a representative commodity (*C*) are

$$\frac{D_c}{\overline{D}_c} = Constant \left(\frac{p_t}{\overline{p}_t}\right)^{\beta_{ct}} \left(\frac{p_p}{\overline{p}_p}\right)^{\beta_{cp}} \left(\frac{p_k}{\overline{p}_k}\right)^{\beta_{ck}} (\cdots)$$

$$\times \left(\frac{p_b}{\overline{p}_b}\right)^{\beta_{cb}} \left(\frac{p_c}{\overline{p}_c}\right)^{\beta_{cc}} \left(\frac{p_d}{\overline{p}_d}\right)^{\beta_{cd}} (\cdots); \quad (94)$$

$$\frac{D_c}{\overline{D}_c} = Constant \left(\frac{p_t}{\overline{p}_t}\right)^{\beta_{ct}} \left(\frac{p_p}{\overline{p}_p}\right)^{\beta_{cp}} \left(\frac{p_k}{\overline{p}_k}\right)^{\beta_{ck}} (\cdots)$$

$$\times \left(\frac{p_b}{\overline{p}_b}\right)^{\beta_{cb}} \left(\frac{p_c}{\overline{p}_c}\right)^{\beta_{cc}} \left(\frac{p_d}{\overline{p}_d}\right)^{\beta_{cd}} (\cdots)$$

$$\times e^{\beta'_{ct}\left(\frac{p_t}{\overline{p}_t}\right) + \beta'_{cp}\left(\frac{p_p}{\overline{p}_p}\right) + \cdots + \beta'_{cd}\left(\frac{p_d}{\overline{p}_d}\right) + \cdots}; \quad (95)$$

$$\frac{D_c}{\overline{D}_c} = Constant \left(\frac{p_t}{\overline{p}_t}\right)^{\beta_{ct}} \left(\frac{p_p}{\overline{p}_p}\right)^{\beta_{cp}} \left(\frac{p_k}{\overline{p}_k}\right)^{\beta_{ck}} (\cdots)$$

$$\times \left(\frac{p_b}{\overline{p}_b}\right)^{\beta_{cb}} \left(\frac{p_c}{\overline{p}_c}\right)^{\beta_{cc}} \left(\frac{p_d}{\overline{p}_d}\right)^{\beta_{cd}} (\cdots)$$

$$\times e^{\left[\beta'_{ct}\left(\frac{p_t}{\overline{p}_t}\right) + \beta'_{cp}\left(\frac{p_p}{\overline{p}_p}\right) + \cdots + \beta'_{cd}\left(\frac{p_d}{\overline{p}_d}\right) + \cdots\right]}$$

$$\times e^{\frac{1}{2}\left[\beta''_{ct}\left(\frac{p_t}{\overline{p}_t}\right)^2 + \beta''_{cp}\left(\frac{p_p}{\overline{p}_p}\right)^2 + \cdots\right]}. \quad (96)$$

These functions may be simplified by a convention which we shall adopt, not only for the functions of demand, but also for the supply functions and the production functions. The convention is this: When all of the independent variables have their trend-values, so likewise will the dependent variables have their trend-values. In case of the demand functions this convention means: When all prices have their trend-values, so likewise the quantity demanded will have its trend-value. In harmony with this convention, functions (94), (95), (96) become, respectively,

$$\frac{D_c}{\overline{D}_c} = \left(\frac{p_t}{\overline{p}_t}\right)^{\beta_{ct}} \left(\frac{p_p}{\overline{p}_p}\right)^{\beta_{cp}} \left(\frac{p_k}{\overline{p}_k}\right)^{\beta_{ck}} (\cdots)$$
$$\times \left(\frac{p_b}{\overline{p}_b}\right)^{\beta_{cb}} \left(\frac{p_c}{\overline{p}_c}\right)^{\beta_{cc}} \left(\frac{p_d}{\overline{p}_d}\right)^{\beta_{cd}} (\cdots); \quad (97)$$

$$\frac{D_c}{\overline{D}_c} = \left(\frac{p_t}{\overline{p}_t}\right)^{\beta_{ct}} \left(\frac{p_p}{\overline{p}_p}\right)^{\beta_{cp}} \left(\frac{p_k}{\overline{p}_k}\right)^{\beta_{ck}} (\cdots)$$
$$\times \left(\frac{p_b}{\overline{p}_b}\right)^{\beta_{cb}} \left(\frac{p_c}{\overline{p}_c}\right)^{\beta_{cc}} \left(\frac{p_d}{\overline{p}_d}\right)^{\beta_{cd}} (\cdots)$$
$$\times e^{\beta'_{ct}\left(\frac{p_t}{\overline{p}_t}-1\right)+\beta'_{cp}\left(\frac{p_p}{\overline{p}_p}-1\right)+\beta'_{ck}\left(\frac{p_k}{\overline{p}_k}-1\right)+\cdots}; \quad (98)$$

$$\frac{D_c}{\overline{D}_c} = \left(\frac{p_t}{\overline{p}_t}\right)^{\beta_{ct}} \left(\frac{p_p}{\overline{p}_p}\right)^{\beta_{cp}} \left(\frac{p_k}{\overline{p}_k}\right)^{\beta_{ck}} (\cdots)$$
$$\times \left(\frac{p_b}{\overline{p}_b}\right)^{\beta_{cb}} \left(\frac{p_c}{\overline{p}_c}\right)^{\beta_{cc}} \left(\frac{p_d}{\overline{p}_d}\right)^{\beta_{cd}} (\cdots)$$
$$\times e^{\beta'_{ct}\left(\frac{p_t}{\overline{p}_t}-1\right)+\beta'_{cp}\left(\frac{p_p}{\overline{p}_p}-1\right)+\beta'_{ck}\left(\frac{p_k}{\overline{p}_k}-1\right)+\cdots}$$
$$\times e^{\frac{1}{2}\left\{\beta''_{ct}\left[\left(\frac{p_t}{\overline{p}_t}\right)^2-1\right]+\beta''_{cp}\left[\left(\frac{p_p}{\overline{p}_p}\right)^2-1\right]+\beta''_{ck}\left[\left(\frac{p_k}{\overline{p}_k}\right)^2-1\right]+\cdots\right\}}. \quad (99)$$

Let us observe before going on to deal with the supply functions and the production functions that, reasonable as this convention is, we could avoid making use of it, if there were need, by changing the character of our typical functions. In the first section of this chapter, "A Moving Particular Equilibrium of Demand and Supply," we found, when the trends of prices and quantities of commodities are fitted to the respective raw data by the method of least squares, the mean values of the price trend-ratios and the mean values of the quantity trend-ratios are, within the limit of allowable error, each equal to unity. Moreover, we know that linear functions fitted to data by the method of least squares are satisfied by the mean values of the variables. If, therefore, we take our typical function of demand, typical function of supply, and typical function of production in the linear form

$$y = a_0 + a_1x_1 + a_2x_2 + a_3x_3 + \cdots,$$

where the y's and x's are trend-ratios, then

$$\bar{y} = a_0 + a_1\bar{x}_1 + a_2\bar{x}_2 + a_3\bar{x}_3 + \cdots$$

is a true equation if the $\bar{y}$'s and $\bar{x}$'s are the mean values of the y's and x's. The significance for our problem of this characteristic of linear functions fitted to data by the method of least squares is clear. Since the mean values of our trend-ratios of prices and our trend-ratios of quantities of commodities are, in each case, unity, the constants in the typical equation

$$y = a_0 + a_1x_1 + a_2x_2 + a_3x_3 + \cdots$$

have such values that when the x's are all equal to unity, y is equal to unity.[14]

[14] If the typical functions are taken in the form

$$y = a_0 + a_1x_1 + a_2x_2 + a_3x_3 + \cdots$$

the question will arise as to the economic significance of the a-coefficients. For demand functions of this type, these coefficients are the values of the respective partial elasticities of demand when the variables have their trend values; for the supply functions, they are the respective partial elasticities of supply when the variables have their trend values; and for the production functions, they are the respective partial efficiencies of organization when the variables have their trend values. The method of proof would be the same in all three cases, but we shall give it only for the demand functions. The demand function for commodity (C), if taken in the above form, would be

$$\frac{D_c}{\bar{D}_c} = a_0 + a_1\left(\frac{p_1}{\bar{p}_1}\right) + a_2\left(\frac{p_2}{\bar{p}_2}\right) + a_3\left(\frac{p_3}{\bar{p}_3}\right) + \cdots.$$

The partial elasticity of demand for (C) with respect to a representative

Returning, now, to the question of simplifying our real functions, we may consider the three supply functions developed in Chapter IV on "The Law of Supply." These three functions for the supply of a representative service (T) become, by the use of the convention which we have just employed when treating demand functions,

$$\frac{S_t}{\overline{S}_t} = \left(\frac{p_t}{\overline{p}_t}\right)^{\gamma_{tt}} \left(\frac{p_p}{\overline{p}_p}\right)^{\gamma_{tp}} \left(\frac{p_k}{\overline{p}_k}\right)^{\gamma_{tk}} (\cdots)$$
$$\times \left(\frac{p_b}{\overline{p}_b}\right)^{\gamma_{tb}} \left(\frac{p_c}{\overline{p}_c}\right)^{\gamma_{tc}} \left(\frac{p_d}{\overline{p}_d}\right)^{\gamma_{td}} (\cdots); \quad (100)$$

$$\frac{S_t}{\overline{S}_t} = \left(\frac{p_t}{\overline{p}_t}\right)^{\gamma_{tt}} \left(\frac{p_p}{\overline{p}_p}\right)^{\gamma_{tp}} \left(\frac{p_k}{\overline{p}_k}\right)^{\gamma_{tk}} (\cdots)$$
$$\times \left(\frac{p_b}{\overline{p}_b}\right)^{\gamma_{tb}} \left(\frac{p_c}{\overline{p}_c}\right)^{\gamma_{tc}} \left(\frac{p_d}{\overline{p}_d}\right)^{\gamma_{td}} (\cdots)$$
$$\times e^{\gamma'_{tt}\left(\frac{p_t}{p_t}-1\right)+\gamma'_{tp}\left(\frac{p_p}{p_p}-1\right)+\gamma'_{tk}\left(\frac{p_k}{p_k}-1\right)+\cdots}; \quad (101)$$

$$\frac{S_t}{\overline{S}_t} = \left(\frac{p_t}{\overline{p}_t}\right)^{\gamma_{tt}} \left(\frac{p_p}{\overline{p}_p}\right)^{\gamma_{tp}} \left(\frac{p_k}{\overline{p}_k}\right)^{\gamma_{tk}} (\cdots)$$
$$\times \left(\frac{p_b}{\overline{p}_b}\right)^{\gamma_{tb}} \left(\frac{p_c}{\overline{p}_c}\right)^{\gamma_{tc}} \left(\frac{p_d}{\overline{p}_d}\right)^{\gamma_{td}} (\cdots)$$
$$\times e^{\gamma'_{tt}\left(\frac{p_t}{p_t}-1\right)+\gamma'_{tp}\left(\frac{p_p}{p_p}-1\right)+\gamma'_{tk}\left(\frac{p_k}{p_k}-1\right)+\cdots}$$
$$\times e^{\frac{1}{2}\left\{\gamma''_{tt}\left[\left(\frac{p_t}{p_t}\right)^2-1\right]+\gamma''_{tp}\left[\left(\frac{p_p}{p_p}\right)^2-1\right]+\gamma''_{tk}\left[\left(\frac{p_k}{p_k}\right)^2-1\right]+\cdots\right\}}. \quad (102)$$

price, p_1, is, according to the definition of partial elasticity of demand given in Chapter III,

$$\eta_{cp_1 \cdot p_2 p_3 p_4 \cdots} = \frac{p_1}{D_c} \cdot \frac{\partial D_c}{\partial p_1}.$$

But

$$\frac{\partial D_c}{\partial p_1} = a_1 \frac{\overline{D}_c}{\overline{p}_1},$$

and consequently, when $p_1 = \overline{p}_1$ and $D_c = \overline{D}_c$, we have

$$\eta_{cp_1 \cdot p_2 p_3 p_4 \cdots} = a_1.$$

By the use of the same convention, the three production functions developed in Chapter IV are, for the representative commodity (C),

$$\frac{Q_c}{\overline{Q}_c} = \left(\frac{T_c}{\overline{T}_c}\right)^{\epsilon_{ct}} \left(\frac{P_c}{\overline{P}_c}\right)^{\epsilon_{cp}} \left(\frac{K_c}{\overline{K}_c}\right)^{\epsilon_{ck}} (\cdots); \qquad (103)$$

$$\frac{Q_c}{\overline{Q}_c} = \left(\frac{T_c}{\overline{T}_c}\right)^{\epsilon_{ct}} \left(\frac{P_c}{\overline{P}_c}\right)^{\epsilon_{cp}} \left(\frac{K_c}{\overline{K}_c}\right)^{\epsilon_{ck}} (\cdots)$$
$$\times \ e^{\epsilon'_{ct}\left(\frac{T_c}{\overline{T}_c}-1\right)+\epsilon'_{cp}\left(\frac{P_c}{\overline{P}_c}-1\right)+\epsilon'_{ck}\left(\frac{K_c}{\overline{K}_c}-1\right)+\cdots}; \quad (104)$$

$$\frac{Q_c}{\overline{Q}_c} = \left(\frac{T_c}{\overline{T}_c}\right)^{\epsilon_{ct}} \left(\frac{P_c}{\overline{P}_c}\right)^{\epsilon_{cp}} \left(\frac{K_c}{\overline{K}_c}\right)^{\epsilon_{ck}} (\cdots)$$
$$\times \ e^{\epsilon'_{ct}\left(\frac{T_c}{\overline{T}_c}-1\right)+\epsilon'_{cp}\left(\frac{P_c}{\overline{P}_c}-1\right)+\epsilon'_{ck}\left(\frac{K_c}{\overline{K}_c}-1\right)+\cdots}$$
$$\times \ e^{\frac{1}{2}\left\{\epsilon''_{ct}\left[\left(\frac{T_c}{\overline{T}_c}\right)^2-1\right]+\epsilon''_{cp}\left[\left(\frac{P_c}{\overline{P}_c}\right)^2-1\right]+\epsilon''_{ck}\left[\left(\frac{K_c}{\overline{K}_c}\right)^2-1\right]+\cdots\right\}}. \quad (105)$$

Coefficients of Production

The concrete production functions (103), (104), (105) afford the means of computing the coefficients of production as constants, or as linear functions of the respective factors of production, or as quadratic functions of the respective factors.

Before proceeding with the demonstration let us recall the meaning of the symbols. In the chapter on "The Law of Supply" we began with the abstract production function

$$Q_c = \Psi(P_c) \qquad (106)$$

in which Q_c represents the quantity produced of commodity (C), and P_c is the quantity of service of persons needed in the production. For the sake of simplicity of exposition we assumed that services of persons alone were needed as a factor of production. We then defined relative efficiency of organization as the ratio of the relative change in the quantity of commodity produced to the relative change in the factor of production. If ω is put for the relative efficiency of organization, the symbolic expression of this conception becomes, for the representative commodity (C),

$$\omega = \frac{dQ_c}{Q_c} \bigg/ \frac{dP_c}{P_c} = \frac{P_c}{Q_c} \cdot \frac{dQ_c}{dP_c} . \qquad (107)$$

If, now, the abstract production function is taken in the form

$$Q_c = \Psi(T_c \cdots, P_c \cdots, K_c \cdots, \cdots), \qquad (108)$$

in which the factors of production are the services of land, T_c, T_c', T_c'', $\cdots$, services of persons, P_c, P_c', P_c'', $\cdots$, and services of capital, K_c, K_c', K_c'', $\cdots$, the preceding reasoning suggests that there is a partial relative efficiency of organization with respect to each of the factors of production. By analogy with the definition in (107) we wrote, in Chapter IV, these partial relative efficiencies of organization as

$$\left.\begin{array}{l} \omega_{ct \cdot pk\cdots} = \dfrac{T_c}{Q_c} \cdot \dfrac{\partial Q_c}{\partial T_c}, \\[2ex] \omega_{cp \cdot tk\cdots} = \dfrac{P_c}{Q_c} \cdot \dfrac{\partial Q_c}{\partial P_c}, \\[2ex] \omega_{ck \cdot tp\cdots} = \dfrac{K_c}{Q_c} \cdot \dfrac{\partial Q_c}{\partial K_c}, \\[1ex] \cdot \quad \cdot \quad \cdot \quad \cdot \quad \cdot \quad \cdot \quad \cdot \end{array}\right\} \qquad (109)$$

The quantities T_c/Q_c, P_c/Q_c, K_c/Q_c, $\cdots$, which appear in (109), are Walras' coefficients of production. In Walras' notation {see equation (92)}, $T_c/Q_c = c_t$; $P_c/Q_c = c_p$; $K_c/Q_c = c_k$. By utilizing equation (109), these coefficients of production may be written

$$
\left.\begin{aligned}
c_t &= \omega_{ct \cdot pk\cdots} \Big/ \frac{\partial Q_c}{\partial T_c}, \\[2mm]
c_p &= \omega_{cp \cdot tk\cdots} \Big/ \frac{\partial Q_c}{\partial P_c}, \\[2mm]
c_k &= \omega_{ck \cdot tp\cdots} \Big/ \frac{\partial Q_c}{\partial K_c}.
\end{aligned}\right\}
\qquad (110)
$$

The expressions in (110) make clear that the c's may be calculated if we can find the concrete values of the two factors of which the c's are quotients.

We now see how the concrete production functions (103), (104), (105) supply an indispensable element in the computation of the coefficients of production. Equation (103) gives the partial relative efficiencies of organization as constants. The evaluation of the parameters in (103) leads to

$$
\left.\begin{aligned}
\omega_{ct \cdot pk\cdots} &= \epsilon_{ct}, \\
\omega_{cp \cdot tk\cdots} &= \epsilon_{cp}, \\
\omega_{ck \cdot tp\cdots} &= \epsilon_{ck}, \\
\cdots\;\cdots\;\cdots &
\end{aligned}\right\}
\qquad (111)
$$

The computation of the parameters in (104) gives the partial relative efficiencies as linear functions of the respective factors of production:

$$
\left.\begin{aligned}
\omega_{ct \cdot pk\cdots} &= \epsilon_{ct} + \epsilon'_{ct}\left(\frac{T_c}{\overline{T}_c}\right), \\[2mm]
\omega_{cp \cdot tk\cdots} &= \epsilon_{cp} + \epsilon'_{cp}\left(\frac{P_c}{\overline{P}_c}\right), \\[2mm]
\omega_{ck \cdot tp\cdots} &= \epsilon_{ck} + \epsilon'_{ck}\left(\frac{K_c}{\overline{K}_c}\right), \\[2mm]
\cdots\;\cdots\;\cdots\;\cdots\;\cdots &
\end{aligned}\right\}
\qquad (112)
$$

The evaluation of the parameters in (105) gives the partial relative efficiencies as quadratic functions of the respective factors:

$$\left.\begin{aligned}
\omega_{ct \cdot pk \cdots} &= \epsilon_{ct} + \epsilon_{ct}'\left(\frac{T_c}{\overline{T}_c}\right) + \epsilon_{ct}''\left(\frac{T_c}{\overline{T}_c}\right)^2, \\
\omega_{cp \cdot tk \cdots} &= \epsilon_{cp} + \epsilon_{cp}'\left(\frac{P_c}{\overline{P}_c}\right) + \epsilon_{cp}''\left(\frac{P_c}{\overline{P}_c}\right)^2, \\
\omega_{ck \cdot tp \cdots} &= \epsilon_{ck} + \epsilon_{ck}'\left(\frac{K_c}{\overline{K}_c}\right) + \epsilon_{ck}''\left(\frac{K_c}{\overline{K}_c}\right)^2, \\
&\cdot \quad \cdot \quad \cdot \quad \cdot \quad \cdot \quad \cdot \quad \cdot \quad \cdot \quad \cdot \quad \cdot \quad \cdot \quad \cdot
\end{aligned}\right\} \quad (113)$$

By substituting in (110) the concrete values of the ω's supplied, respectively, by (111), (112), (113), we obtain three groups of equations that give the values of the c's with increasing accuracy. These three groups are:

$$\left.\begin{aligned}
c_t &= \epsilon_{ct}\bigg/\frac{\partial Q_c}{\partial T_c}, \\
c_p &= \epsilon_{cp}\bigg/\frac{\partial Q_c}{\partial P_c}, \\
c_k &= \epsilon_{ck}\bigg/\frac{\partial Q_c}{\partial K_c}, \\
&\cdot \quad \cdot \quad \cdot \quad \cdot \quad \cdot
\end{aligned}\right\} \quad (114)$$

$$\left.\begin{aligned}
c_t &= \left[\epsilon_{ct} + \epsilon_{ct}'\left(\frac{T_c}{\overline{T}_c}\right)\right]\bigg/\frac{\partial Q_c}{\partial T_c}, \\
c_p &= \left[\epsilon_{cp} + \epsilon_{cp}'\left(\frac{P_c}{\overline{P}_c}\right)\right]\bigg/\frac{\partial Q_c}{\partial P_c}, \\
c_k &= \left[\epsilon_{ck} + \epsilon_{ck}'\left(\frac{K_c}{\overline{K}_c}\right)\right]\bigg/\frac{\partial Q_c}{\partial K_c}, \\
&\cdot \quad \cdot \quad \cdot \quad \cdot \quad \cdot \quad \cdot \quad \cdot \quad \cdot \quad \cdot
\end{aligned}\right\} \quad (115)$$

$$c_t = \left[\epsilon_{ct} + \epsilon'_{ct}\left(\frac{T_c}{\overline{T}_c}\right) + \epsilon''_{ct}\left(\frac{T_c}{\overline{T}_c}\right)^2 \right] \Big/ \frac{\partial Q_c}{\partial T_c},$$

$$c_p = \left[\epsilon_{cp} + \epsilon'_{cp}\left(\frac{P_c}{\overline{P}_c}\right) + \epsilon''_{cp}\left(\frac{P_c}{\overline{P}_c}\right)^2 \right] \Big/ \frac{\partial Q_c}{\partial P_c}, \qquad (116)$$

$$c_k = \left[\epsilon_{ck} + \epsilon'_{ck}\left(\frac{K_c}{\overline{K}_c}\right) + \epsilon''_{ck}\left(\frac{K_c}{\overline{K}_c}\right)^2 \right] \Big/ \frac{\partial Q_c}{\partial K_c},$$

. . . .

We have now to come to a decision as to the best values to give to the partial derivatives on the right-hand side of (114), (115), (116). Economic theory supplies a clue to the solution of the problem. According to the productivity theory of distribution, the utilization of each factor in production is carried to the point where the value of the product imputed to the final increment of the factor is just equal to the price of the increment of the factor. This theory would require in the present circumstances [15] that

$$\frac{\partial Q_c}{\partial T_c} \cdot \Delta T_c \cdot p_c = \Delta T_c \cdot p_t,$$

$$\frac{\partial Q_c}{\partial P_c} \cdot \Delta P_c \cdot p_c = \Delta P_c \cdot p_p, \qquad (117)$$

$$\frac{\partial Q_c}{\partial K_c} \cdot \Delta K_c \cdot p_c = \Delta K_c \cdot p_k.$$

Equations (117) become, by an obvious simplification,

$$\frac{\partial Q_c}{\partial T_c} = \frac{p_t}{p_c},$$

$$\frac{\partial Q_c}{\partial P_c} = \frac{p_p}{p_c}, \qquad (118)$$

$$\frac{\partial Q_c}{\partial K_c} = \frac{p_k}{p_c}.$$

[15] Walras: *Note sur la réfutation de la théorie anglaise du fermage de M. Wicksteed.* Lausanne, 1896, p. 10.

There is a condition implied in the productivity theory of distribution of which notice must be taken before equations (118), which have been reached through the application of the productivity theory, can be put into their final shape. The productivity theory postulates a condition of equilibrium. The prices of the marginal products are equal to the prices of the responsible marginal factors only when production has reached the stage of minimum cost, which is a stage of theoretical equilibrium. In order that equations (118) may be true to the implicit assumption of equilibrium, the p's must be given the values that would be attained in a state of equilibrium.

What are the most probable values that should be assigned to the p's? The method we have followed in the derivation of the empirical laws of demand and the empirical laws of supply throws light on the question. The typical laws of demand derived in Chapter III are here reproduced as equations (97), (98), (99); the typical laws of supply, as equations (100), (101), (102). In both of these cases we found that the average of the price trend-ratios $(p/\bar{p})$ is unity. Consequently, on an average, at any particular time, the most probable value of p is its trend-value $\bar{p}$. If we assume that these average, most probable values are the values toward which the forces at work are urging the movement of prices, we may substitute them for the equilibrium prices postulated in the productivity theory. If these substitutions are made, equations (118) become:

$$\frac{\partial Q_c}{\partial T_c} = \frac{\bar{p}_t}{\bar{p}_c},$$

$$\frac{\partial Q_c}{\partial P_c} = \frac{\bar{p}_p}{\bar{p}_c}, \tag{119}$$

$$\frac{\partial Q_c}{\partial K_c} = \frac{\bar{p}_k}{\bar{p}_c}.$$

The coefficients of production may now be determined as constants, or as linear functions of the respective factors of production, or as quadratic functions of the respective factors. By substituting in (114) the values of the partial derivatives in (119), we obtain coefficients of production in which the partial relative efficiencies of organization are constants:

$$c_t = \epsilon_{ct} \frac{\bar{p}_c}{\bar{p}_t},$$

$$c_p = \epsilon_{cp} \frac{\bar{p}_c}{\bar{p}_p}, \tag{120}$$

$$c_k = \epsilon_{ck} \frac{\bar{p}_c}{\bar{p}_k}.$$

By substituting in (115), we obtain the coefficients of production as linear functions of the respective factors of production:

$$c_t = \left[\epsilon_{ct} + \epsilon'_{ct}\left(\frac{T_c}{\bar{T}_c}\right) \right] \cdot \frac{\bar{p}_c}{\bar{p}_t},$$

$$c_p = \left[\epsilon_{cp} + \epsilon'_{cp}\left(\frac{P_c}{\bar{P}_c}\right) \right] \cdot \frac{\bar{p}_c}{\bar{p}_p}, \tag{121}$$

$$c_k = \left[\epsilon_{ck} + \epsilon'_{ck}\left(\frac{K_c}{\bar{K}_c}\right) \right] \cdot \frac{\bar{p}_c}{\bar{p}_k}.$$

By substituting in (116), we obtain the coefficients of

production as quadratic functions of the respective factors of production:

$$c_t = \left[\epsilon_{ct} + \epsilon'_{ct}\left(\frac{T_c}{\overline{T}_c}\right) + \epsilon''_{ct}\left(\frac{T_c}{\overline{T}_c}\right)^2 \right] \cdot \frac{\overline{p}_c}{\overline{p}_t},$$

$$c_p = \left[\epsilon_{cp} + \epsilon'_{cp}\left(\frac{P_c}{\overline{P}_c}\right) + \epsilon''_{cp}\left(\frac{P_c}{\overline{P}_c}\right)^2 \right] \cdot \frac{\overline{p}_c}{\overline{p}_p}, \qquad (122)$$

$$c_k = \left[\epsilon_{ck} + \epsilon'_{ck}\left(\frac{K_c}{\overline{K}_c}\right) + \epsilon''_{ck}\left(\frac{K_c}{\overline{K}_c}\right)^2 \right] \cdot \frac{\overline{p}_c}{\overline{p}_k}.$$

A Moving General Equilibrium: First Approximation

We have now the means by which to pass from Walras' hypothetical, statical general equilibrium to a real, moving general equilibrium. Walras' problem is solved by means of his four groups of equations (90), (91), (92), (93), all of which are hypothetical and apply only to his theoretical, static state. For each of his groups we may now substitute equations that may be statistically evaluated and that apply to the actual changing economy.

In place of Walras' hypothetical demand equations (90) we substitute concrete demand equations of type (97), or (98), or (99), which reproduce the partial elasticities of demand as constants, or as linear functions of the respective prices, or as quadratic functions of the prices. The three types are:

$$
\left.
\begin{aligned}
\frac{D_c}{\overline{D}_c} &= \left(\frac{p_t}{\overline{p}_t}\right)^{\beta_{ct}} \left(\frac{p_p}{\overline{p}_p}\right)^{\beta_{cp}} \left(\frac{p_k}{\overline{p}_k}\right)^{\beta_{ck}} (\ldots) \\
&\qquad \times \left(\frac{p_b}{\overline{p}_b}\right)^{\beta_{cb}} \left(\frac{p_c}{\overline{p}_c}\right)^{\beta_{cc}} \left(\frac{p_d}{\overline{p}_d}\right)^{\beta_{cd}} (\ldots), \\[4pt]
\frac{D_c}{\overline{D}_c} &= \left(\frac{p_t}{\overline{p}_t}\right)^{\beta_{ct}} \left(\frac{p_p}{\overline{p}_p}\right)^{\beta_{cp}} \left(\frac{p_k}{\overline{p}_k}\right)^{\beta_{ck}} (\ldots) \\
&\qquad \times \left(\frac{p_b}{\overline{p}_b}\right)^{\beta_{cb}} \left(\frac{p_c}{\overline{p}_c}\right)^{\beta_{cc}} \left(\frac{p_d}{\overline{p}_d}\right)^{\beta_{cd}} (\ldots) \\
&\qquad \times e^{\beta'_{ct}\left(\frac{p_t}{\overline{p}_t}-1\right)+\beta'_{cp}\left(\frac{p_p}{\overline{p}_p}-1\right)+\beta'_{ck}\left(\frac{p_k}{\overline{p}_k}-1\right)+\cdots}, \\[4pt]
\frac{D_c}{\overline{D}_c} &= \left(\frac{p_t}{\overline{p}_t}\right)^{\beta_{ct}} \left(\frac{p_p}{\overline{p}_p}\right)^{\beta_{cp}} \left(\frac{p_k}{\overline{p}_k}\right)^{\beta_{ck}} (\ldots) \\
&\qquad \times \left(\frac{p_b}{\overline{p}_b}\right)^{\beta_{cb}} \left(\frac{p_c}{\overline{p}_c}\right)^{\beta_{cc}} \left(\frac{p_d}{\overline{p}_d}\right)^{\beta_{cd}} (\ldots) \\
&\qquad \times e^{\beta'_{ct}\left(\frac{p_t}{\overline{p}_t}-1\right)+\beta'_{cp}\left(\frac{p_p}{\overline{p}_p}-1\right)+\beta'_{ck}\left(\frac{p_k}{\overline{p}_k}-1\right)+\cdots} \\
&\qquad \times e^{\frac{1}{2}\left\{\beta''_{ct}\left[\left(\frac{p_t}{\overline{p}_t}\right)^2-1\right]+\beta''_{cp}\left[\left(\frac{p_p}{\overline{p}_p}\right)^2-1\right]+\beta''_{ck}\left[\left(\frac{p_k}{\overline{p}_k}\right)^2-1\right]+\cdots\right\}}
\end{aligned}
\right\} \quad (123)
$$

In place of Walras' hypothetical supply equations (91) we substitute concrete supply equations of type (100), or (101), or (102), which reproduce the partial elasticities of supply as constants, or as linear functions of the respective prices, or as quadratic functions of the prices. The three types are:

$$
\left.
\begin{aligned}
\frac{S_t}{\overline{S}_t} &= \left(\frac{p_t}{\overline{p}_t}\right)^{\gamma_{tt}} \left(\frac{p_p}{\overline{p}_p}\right)^{\gamma_{tp}} \left(\frac{p_k}{\overline{p}_k}\right)^{\gamma_{tk}} (\ldots) \\
&\qquad \times \left(\frac{p_b}{\overline{p}_b}\right)^{\gamma_{tb}} \left(\frac{p_c}{\overline{p}_c}\right)^{\gamma_{tc}} \left(\frac{p_d}{\overline{p}_d}\right)^{\gamma_{td}} (\ldots), \\[4pt]
\frac{S_t}{\overline{S}_t} &= \left(\frac{p_t}{\overline{p}_t}\right)^{\gamma_{tt}} \left(\frac{p_p}{\overline{p}_p}\right)^{\gamma_{tp}} \left(\frac{p_k}{\overline{p}_k}\right)^{\gamma_{tk}} (\ldots) \\
&\qquad \times \left(\frac{p_b}{\overline{p}_b}\right)^{\gamma_{tb}} \left(\frac{p_c}{\overline{p}_c}\right)^{\gamma_{tc}} \left(\frac{p_d}{\overline{p}_d}\right)^{\gamma_{td}} (\ldots) \\
&\qquad \times e^{\gamma'_{tt}\left(\frac{p_t}{\overline{p}_t}-1\right)+\gamma'_{tp}\left(\frac{p_p}{\overline{p}_p}-1\right)+\gamma'_{tk}\left(\frac{p_k}{\overline{p}_k}-1\right)+\cdots},
\end{aligned}
\right\} \quad (124)
$$

$$\frac{S_t}{\overline{S}_t} = \left(\frac{p_t}{\overline{p}_t}\right)^{\gamma_{tt}} \left(\frac{p_p}{\overline{p}_p}\right)^{\gamma_{tp}} \left(\frac{p_k}{\overline{p}_k}\right)^{\gamma_{tk}} (\cdots)$$

$$\times \left(\frac{p_b}{\overline{p}_b}\right)^{\gamma_{tb}} \left(\frac{p_c}{\overline{p}_c}\right)^{\gamma_{tc}} \left(\frac{p_d}{\overline{p}_d}\right)^{\gamma_{td}} (\cdots)$$

$$\times e^{\gamma'_{tt}\left(\frac{p_t}{\overline{p}_t}-1\right)+\gamma'_{tp}\left(\frac{p_p}{\overline{p}_p}-1\right)+\gamma'_{tk}\left(\frac{p_k}{\overline{p}_k}-1\right)+\cdots}$$

$$\times e^{\frac{1}{2}\left\{\gamma''_{tt}\left[\left(\frac{p_t}{\overline{p}_t}\right)^2-1\right]+\gamma''_{tp}\left[\left(\frac{p_p}{\overline{p}_p}\right)^2-1\right]+\gamma''_{tk}\left[\left(\frac{p_k}{\overline{p}_k}\right)^2-1\right]+\cdots\right\}}.$$

In place of the hypothetical constant coefficients of production by means of which Walras expresses the equation of demand and supply (92), we substitute concrete varying coefficients of production (120), (121), (122), in which the partial relative efficiencies of organization are reproduced as constants, or as linear functions of the respective factors of production, or as quadratic functions of the factors. The three types are:

$$\epsilon_{at}\frac{\overline{p}_a}{\overline{p}_t}D_a + \epsilon_{bt}\frac{\overline{p}_b}{\overline{p}_t}D_b + \epsilon_{ct}\frac{\overline{p}_c}{\overline{p}_t}D_c + \cdots = S_t,$$

$$\left[\epsilon_{at} + \epsilon'_{at}\left(\frac{T_a}{\overline{T}_a}\right)\right]\frac{\overline{p}_a}{\overline{p}_t}D_a$$

$$+ \left[\epsilon_{bt} + \epsilon'_{bt}\left(\frac{T_b}{\overline{T}_b}\right)\right]\frac{\overline{p}_b}{\overline{p}_t}D_b$$

$$+ \left[\epsilon_{ct} + \epsilon'_{ct}\left(\frac{T_c}{\overline{T}_c}\right)\right]\frac{\overline{p}_c}{\overline{p}_t}D_c + \cdots = S_t, \qquad (125)$$

$$\left[\epsilon_{at} + \epsilon'_{at}\left(\frac{T_a}{\overline{T}_a}\right) + \epsilon''_{at}\left(\frac{T_a}{\overline{T}_a}\right)^2\right]\frac{\overline{p}_a}{\overline{p}_t}D_a$$

$$+ \left[\epsilon_{bt} + \epsilon'_{bt}\left(\frac{T_b}{\overline{T}_b}\right)\right.$$

$$\left. + \epsilon''_{bt}\left(\frac{T_b}{\overline{T}_b}\right)^2\right]\frac{\overline{p}_b}{\overline{p}_t}D_b + \cdots = S_t.$$

In place of Walras' equations of cost and price (93), which depend upon the assumption of hypothetical, constant coefficients of production, we substitute others containing real coefficients of production (120), (121), (122), of which the three types are:

$$\left.\begin{array}{l} \epsilon_{ct}\dfrac{\overline{p}_c}{\overline{p}_t}p_t + \epsilon_{cp}\dfrac{\overline{p}_c}{\overline{p}_p}p_p + \epsilon_{ck}\dfrac{\overline{p}_c}{\overline{p}_k}p_k + \cdots = p_c, \\[2ex] \left[\epsilon_{ct} + \epsilon'_{ct}\left(\dfrac{T_c}{\overline{T}_c}\right)\right]\dfrac{\overline{p}_c}{\overline{p}_t}p_t \\[2ex] \qquad + \left[\epsilon_{cp} + \epsilon'_{cp}\left(\dfrac{P_c}{\overline{P}_c}\right)\right]\dfrac{\overline{p}_c}{\overline{p}_p}p_p + \cdots = p_c, \\[2ex] \left[\epsilon_{ct} + \epsilon'_{ct}\left(\dfrac{T_c}{\overline{T}_c}\right) + \epsilon''_{ct}\left(\dfrac{T_c}{\overline{T}_c}\right)^2\right]\dfrac{\overline{p}_c}{\overline{p}_t}p_t \\[2ex] \qquad + \left[\epsilon_{cp} + \epsilon'_{cp}\left(\dfrac{P_c}{\overline{P}_c}\right)\right. \\[2ex] \qquad \left. + \epsilon''_{cp}\left(\dfrac{P_c}{\overline{P}_c}\right)^2\right]\dfrac{\overline{p}_c}{\overline{p}_p}p_p + \cdots = p_c. \end{array}\right\} \quad (126)$$

These four groups of equations (123), (124), (125), (126), like Walras' equations (90), (91), (92), (93), determine a general equilibrium, but the equilibrium with which they are concerned is real and not hypothetic, is moving and not static.

It is a moving equilibrium about the lines of general trend. This may be seen to be true if, in the four groups of representative equations (123), (124), (125), (126), the trend prices are substituted for actual prices. If the trend prices are substituted for actual prices in the typical demand equations (123), D_c becomes $\overline{D}_c$; if they are substituted in the typical supply equations (124), S_t becomes $\bar{S}_t$; the typical equations of demand and supply (125) become: [16]

$$
\left.
\begin{aligned}
&\epsilon_{at}\frac{\bar{p}_a}{\bar{p}_t}\bar{D}_a + \epsilon_{bt}\frac{\bar{p}_b}{\bar{p}_t}\bar{D}_b + \epsilon_{ct}\frac{\bar{p}_c}{\bar{p}_t}\bar{D}_c + \cdots = \bar{S}_t, \\
&(\epsilon_{at} + \epsilon'_{at})\frac{\bar{p}_a}{\bar{p}_t}\bar{D}_a + (\epsilon_{bt} + \epsilon'_{bt})\frac{\bar{p}_b}{\bar{p}_t}\bar{D}_b \\
&\qquad\qquad + (\epsilon_{ct} + \epsilon'_{ct})\frac{\bar{p}_c}{\bar{p}_t}\bar{D}_c + \cdots = \bar{S}_t, \\
&(\epsilon_{at} + \epsilon'_{at} + \epsilon''_{at})\frac{\bar{p}_a}{\bar{p}_t}\bar{D}_a \\
&\qquad + (\epsilon_{bt} + \epsilon'_{bt} + \epsilon''_{bt})\frac{\bar{p}_b}{\bar{p}_t}\bar{D}_b \\
&\qquad + (\epsilon_{ct} + \epsilon'_{ct} + \epsilon''_{ct})\frac{\bar{p}_c}{\bar{p}_t}\bar{D}_c + \cdots = \bar{S}_t.
\end{aligned}
\right\} \quad (127)
$$

and the typical equations of cost and price (126) become:

$$
\left.
\begin{aligned}
&\epsilon_{ct} + \epsilon_{cp} + \epsilon_{ck} + \cdots = 1, \\
&(\epsilon_{ct} + \epsilon'_{ct}) + (\epsilon_{cp} + \epsilon'_{cp}) + (\epsilon_{ck} + \epsilon'_{ck}) + \cdots = 1, \\
&(\epsilon_{ct} + \epsilon'_{ct} + \epsilon''_{ct}) + (\epsilon_{cp} + \epsilon'_{cp} + \epsilon''_{cp}) \\
&\qquad\qquad + (\epsilon_{ck} + \epsilon'_{ck} + \epsilon''_{ck}) + \cdots = 1.
\end{aligned}
\right\} \quad (128)
$$

The Theory of Capitalization

The preceding sections have taken no formal account of the prices of capital goods as distinguished from the prices of the services of those goods; nor of

[16] The fractions $(T/\bar{T})$, $(T/\bar{T})^2$, . . ., which occur in the second and third equations of (125), disappear in the second and third equations of (127). The reason is this: When all price ratios have their mean value, unity, demand ratios $D/\bar{D}$, supply ratios $S/\bar{S}$, and quantity produced ratios $Q/\bar{Q}$ are likewise unity. But from the nature of the production functions (103), (104), (105) we see that the ratio $Q/\bar{Q}$ is equal to unity when $(T/\bar{T})$, $(T/\bar{T})^2$, . . . are equal to unity.

the supply of credit, the rate of interest, and the creation of capital goods; nor of provisions for the insurance and the amortisation of capital goods. The consideration of these elements will introduce new complications into the problem of a moving general equilibrium, but it will bring the mathematical description into a more complete accord with economic facts.

To go forward with the mathematical reasoning we shall have need of additional symbols. The prices of the services of capital goods (K), (K'), (K''), $\cdots$ we have already denoted by p_k, $p_{k'}$, $p_{k''}$, $\cdots$. We shall now symbolize the prices [17] per unit of the capital goods themselves by Π_k, $\Pi_{k'}$, $\Pi_{k''}$, $\cdots$. The mathematical treatment of a moving general equilibrium presupposes that all the elements in the problem refer to a unit of time in which the entrepreneurs balance their budgets. Let us suppose that the amount of credit employed in the unit of time is Γ. The supply of credit, like the supply of services, is a function of all prices, and among these prices we have now to include the price of credit, which is the rate of interest. If i be put for the rate of interest, we may write the law of supply of credit as

$$S_\Gamma = F_\Gamma(p_t, \ p_p, \ p_k, \ \cdots \ p_b, \ p_c, \ p_d, \ \cdots \ i). \quad (129)$$

The rate of insurance may be represented by μ'; the

[17] Walras used P_k, $P_{k'}$, $P_{k''}$, $\cdots$ to represent the prices of capital goods. But he had already employed the letter P to represent services of persons, whence P_k, $P_{k'}$, $P_{k''}$, $\cdots$ would indicate the quantities of P used in the production, respectively, of K, K', K'', $\cdots$. The double meaning of Walras' symbols P_k, $P_{k'}$, $P_{k''}$, $\cdots$ is my reason for departing from his usage and introducing Π_k, $\Pi_{k'}$, $\Pi_{k''}$, $\cdots$ to represent the prices of capital goods.

rate of amortisation by μ''; and for these two together we may write $\mu = \mu' + \mu''$. During the period under investigation there will be need of providing for the physical wear and tear of current capital goods. Let the number of the capital goods necessary for replacement be l'. In course of the same period, capital goods of new types will be produced, which we shall suppose to be l'' in number. The total number of capital goods to be produced in the period will therefore be $l = l' + l''$. Let D_k, $D_{k'}$, $D_{k''}$, $\cdots$ be the respective demands for these l capital goods.

The formal treatment of these new items introduces new equations for the determination of the moving equilibrium. We shall consider first those new equations which have their origin in the relation between the prices of capital goods and the prices of the services of capital goods. Let a representative capital good be (K), of which the price per unit is Π_k and the price for the service of a unit is p_k. In accord with the notation which has been agreed upon, μ_k is the rate of insurance and amortisation per unit of (K). Since (K) is a replaceable capital good, and since the rate of interest is i, the relation between Π_k, p_k, μ_k and i is, in a state of equilibrium,

$$i = \frac{p_k - \mu_k \Pi_k}{\Pi_k}. \qquad (130)$$

In a state of general equilibrium a similar relation must hold for all of the replaceable capital goods, and since there are l of these, of which l' are of current types and l'' of new types, we shall have, for these l capital goods, l equations like equation (130).

The new capital goods must be paid for eventually out of savings, but at a given time the cost may be expressed in terms of credit. The formulation of this relation gives another new equation,

$$D_k\Pi_k + D_{k'}\Pi_{k'} + D_{k''}\Pi_{k''} + \cdots = S_\Gamma. \quad (131)$$

We have now to observe the critical fact that in a condition of equilibrium the above equation (131) expresses a relation between the cost of capital goods and savings. As savings are the difference between income and expenditure for consumption, we have, in a state of equilibrium,

$$[S_t p_t + \cdots + S_p p_p + \cdots + S_k p_k + S_{k'} p_{k'}$$
$$+ S_{k''} p_{k''} + \cdots + S_\Gamma i] - [D_a + D_b p_b$$
$$+ D_c p_c + D_d p_d + \cdots]$$
$$= [D_k\Pi_k + D_{k'}\Pi_{k'} + D_{k''}\Pi_{k''} + \cdots]. \quad (132)$$

The important point to bear in mind is that credit becomes identical with savings in a state of equilibrium.

We may now pass to the consideration of the ensemble of equations determining the moving general equilibrium when savings are made and new capital goods are produced. The first group of these equations is made up of $(m - 1)$ functions of demand for commodities:

$$\left.\begin{array}{l} D_b = F_b(p_t, p_p, p_k, \cdots p_b, p_c, p_d, \cdots i), \\ D_c = F_c(p_t, p_p, p_k, \cdots p_b, p_c, p_d, \cdots i), \\ D_d = F_d(p_t, p_p, p_k, \cdots p_b, p_c, p_d, \cdots i), \\ \cdot \quad \cdot \quad \cdot \quad \cdot \quad \cdot \quad \cdot \quad \cdot \quad \cdot \quad \cdot \quad \cdot \quad \cdot \quad \cdot \quad \cdot \end{array}\right\} \quad (133)$$

These demand functions have as the independent

variables not only all prices but also the rate of interest.

The second group of equations is made up of the n functions of supply of services:

$$\left.\begin{aligned}
S_t &= F_t(p_t,\ p_p,\ p_k,\ \cdots\ p_b,\ p_c,\ p_d,\ \cdots\ i), \\
S_p &= F_p(p_t,\ p_p,\ p_k,\ \cdots\ p_b,\ p_c,\ p_d,\ \cdots\ i), \\
S_k &= F_k(p_t,\ p_p,\ p_k,\ \cdots\ p_b,\ p_c,\ p_d,\ \cdots\ i), \\
&\ \cdot\ \cdot\ \cdot\ \cdot\ \cdot\ \cdot\ \cdot\ \cdot\ \cdot\ \cdot\ \cdot\ \cdot\ \cdot
\end{aligned}\right\} \quad (134)$$

The third group contains only one equation, which is the function of supply of credit:

$$S_\Gamma = F_\Gamma(p_t,\ p_p,\ p_k,\ \cdots\ p_b,\ p_c,\ p_d,\ \cdots\ i). \quad (135)$$

The fourth group is made up of the n equations expressing the equality of the demand for and the supply of production services:

$$\left.\begin{aligned}
a_t D_a + b_t D_b &+ c_t D_c + \cdots \\
&+ k_t D_k + k_t' D_{k'} + k_t'' D_{k''} + \cdots = S_t, \\
a_p D_a + b_p D_b &+ c_p D_c + \cdots \\
&+ k_p D_k + k_p' D_{k'} + k_p'' D_{k''} + \cdots = S_p, \\
a_k D_a + b_k D_b &+ c_k D_c + \cdots \\
&+ k_k D_k + k_k' D_{k'} + k_k'' D_{k''} + \cdots = S_k, \\
&\ \cdot\ \cdot\ \cdot\ \cdot\ \cdot\ \cdot\ \cdot\ \cdot\ \cdot\ \cdot\ \cdot\ \cdot\ \cdot
\end{aligned}\right\} \quad (136)$$

The fifth group consists of the m equations expressing that the prices of the m commodities are equal to their respective costs of production:

$$\left.\begin{aligned}
a_t p_t + a_p p_p + a_k p_k + \cdots &= 1, \\
b_t p_t + b_p p_p + b_k p_k + \cdots &= p_b, \\
c_t p_t + c_p p_p + c_k p_k + \cdots &= p_c, \\
\cdot\ \cdot\ \cdot\ \cdot\ \cdot\ \cdot\ \cdot\ \cdot\ \cdot\ &\cdot
\end{aligned}\right\} \quad (137)$$

The equations of the sixth group express that the prices of the l new capital goods are equal to their respective costs of production:

$$\left.\begin{aligned} k_t p_t + k_p p_p + k_k p_k + \cdots &= \Pi_k, \\ k_t' p_t + k_p' p_p + k_k' p_k + \cdots &= \Pi_{k'}, \\ k_t'' p_t + k_p'' p_p + k_k'' p_k + \cdots &= \Pi_{k''}, \\ \cdot\;\cdot\;\cdot\;\cdot\;\cdot\;\cdot\;\cdot\;\cdot\;\cdot\;\cdot\;\cdot\;\cdot\;\cdot \end{aligned}\right\} \quad (138)$$

The seventh group contains only one equation expressing the equality of the values of the new capital goods and the supply of credit,

$$D_k \Pi_k + D_{k'} \Pi_{k'} + D_{k''} \Pi_{k''} + \cdots = S_r. \quad (139)$$

The eighth group contains l equations expressing the prices of capital goods in terms of the rate of interest and the prices of the services of the respective capital goods:

$$\left.\begin{aligned} \Pi_k &= \frac{p_k}{i + \mu_k}, \\ \Pi_{k'} &= \frac{p_{k'}}{i + \mu_{k'}}, \\ \Pi_{k''} &= \frac{p_{k''}}{i + \mu_{k''}}, \\ \cdot\;\cdot\;\cdot\;\cdot\;\cdot \end{aligned}\right\} \quad (140)$$

These equations are obvious transformations of (130).

A review of these eight groups will show that the number of independent equations is equal to the number of unknown quantities. The unknown quantities are: The m quantities of the m commodities demanded; the $(m - 1)$ prices of the m commodities in terms of one of them which is used as the standard of prices; the n quantities of the n services that are supplied; the n prices of the n services in terms of the standard of prices; the l quantities of the new capital goods; the l prices of the new capital goods; the quantity of credit, which in a state of equilibrium is equal to the amount of savings; the rate of interest. In all there are $(2m + 2n + 2l + 1)$ unknowns. To evaluate these unknowns we have $(2m + 2n + 2l + 1)$ independent equations: The $(m - 1)$ equations of demand for commodities; n equations of supply of services; one function of supply of credit; n equations expressing the equality of the demand for and supply of productive services; m equations expressing that the prices of the m commodities are equal to their respective costs of production; l equations expressing that the prices of the l new capital goods are equal to their respective costs of production; one equation expressing the equality of the value of the new capital goods and credit; l equations expressing the prices of the capital goods in terms of the rate of interest and the prices of the services of capital goods. In all there are $(2m + 2n + 2l + 1)$ independent equations.

A Moving General Equilibrium: Second Approximation

The foregoing theory of equilibrium under conditions of capitalization may be put into a form which will admit of concrete, statistical treatment. A moving general equilibrium will thus be described which will reveal the actual joint determination of the essential facts and laws of exchange, production, capitalization, and distribution.

The first group of equations contributing to the

concrete description of the moving general equilibrium comprises the $(m-1)$ demand functions which, like the demand equations in (123), may in each case take any one of three forms. They differ from the equations in (123) only in the insertion of the interest ratio $(i/\bar{\imath})$ among the independent variables. The three types are:

$$
\left.
\begin{aligned}
\frac{D_c}{\overline{D}_c} &= \left(\frac{p_t}{\overline{p}_t}\right)^{\beta_{ct}} \left(\frac{p_p}{\overline{p}_p}\right)^{\beta_{cp}} \left(\frac{p_k}{\overline{p}_k}\right)^{\beta_{ck}} (\dots) \\
&\quad \times \left(\frac{p_b}{\overline{p}_b}\right)^{\beta_{cb}} \left(\frac{p_c}{\overline{p}_c}\right)^{\beta_{cc}} \left(\frac{p_d}{\overline{p}_d}\right)^{\beta_{cd}} (\dots) \left(\frac{i}{\bar{\imath}}\right)^{\beta_{ci}}, \\[2mm]
\frac{D_c}{\overline{D}_c} &= \left(\frac{p_t}{\overline{p}_t}\right)^{\beta_{ct}} \left(\frac{p_p}{\overline{p}_p}\right)^{\beta_{cp}} \left(\frac{p_k}{\overline{p}_k}\right)^{\beta_{ck}} (\dots) \\
&\quad \times \left(\frac{p_b}{\overline{p}_b}\right)^{\beta_{cb}} \left(\frac{p_c}{\overline{p}_c}\right)^{\beta_{cc}} \left(\frac{p_d}{\overline{p}_d}\right)^{\beta_{cd}} (\dots) \left(\frac{i}{\bar{\imath}}\right)^{\beta_{ci}} \\
&\quad \times e^{\beta'_{ct}\left(\frac{p_t}{\overline{p}_t}-1\right)+\beta'_{cp}\left(\frac{p_p}{\overline{p}_p}-1\right)+\beta'_{ck}\left(\frac{p_k}{\overline{p}_k}-1\right)+\cdots+\beta'_{ci}\left(\frac{i}{\bar{\imath}}-1\right)}, \\[2mm]
\frac{D_c}{\overline{D}_c} &= \left(\frac{p_t}{\overline{p}_t}\right)^{\beta_{ct}} \left(\frac{p_p}{\overline{p}_p}\right)^{\beta_{cp}} \left(\frac{p_k}{\overline{p}_k}\right)^{\beta_{ck}} (\dots) \\
&\quad \times \left(\frac{p_b}{\overline{p}_b}\right)^{\beta_{cb}} \left(\frac{p_c}{\overline{p}_c}\right)^{\beta_{cc}} \left(\frac{p_d}{\overline{p}_d}\right)^{\beta_{cd}} (\dots) \left(\frac{i}{\bar{\imath}}\right)^{\beta_{ci}} \\
&\quad \times e^{\beta'_{ct}\left(\frac{p_t}{\overline{p}_t}-1\right)+\beta'_{cp}\left(\frac{p_p}{\overline{p}_p}-1\right)+\beta'_{ck}\left(\frac{p_k}{\overline{p}_k}-1\right)+\cdots+\beta'_{ci}\left(\frac{i}{\bar{\imath}}-1\right)} \\
&\quad \times e^{\frac{1}{2}\left\{\beta''_{ct}\left[\left(\frac{p_t}{\overline{p}_t}\right)^2-1\right]+\beta''_{cp}\left[\left(\frac{p_p}{\overline{p}_p}\right)^2-1\right]+\cdots+\beta''_{ci}\left[\left(\frac{i}{\bar{\imath}}\right)^2-1\right]\right\}}.
\end{aligned}
\right\} \quad (141)
$$

The second group of equations is made up of the n functions of supply services. These equations are the same as the corresponding supply equations in (124) with the interest ratio $(i/\bar{\imath})$ inserted among the independent variables. The three types are:

$$\frac{S_t}{\bar{S}_t} = \left(\frac{p_t}{\bar{p}_t}\right)^{\gamma_{tt}} \left(\frac{p_p}{\bar{p}_p}\right)^{\gamma_{tp}} \left(\frac{p_k}{\bar{p}_k}\right)^{\gamma_{tk}} (\cdots)$$
$$\times \left(\frac{p_b}{\bar{p}_b}\right)^{\gamma_{tb}} \left(\frac{p_c}{\bar{p}_c}\right)^{\gamma_{tc}} \left(\frac{p_d}{\bar{p}_d}\right)^{\gamma_{td}} (\cdots) \left(\frac{i}{\bar{i}}\right)^{\gamma_{ti}},$$

$$\frac{S_t}{\bar{S}_t} = \left(\frac{p_t}{\bar{p}_t}\right)^{\gamma_{tt}} \left(\frac{p_p}{\bar{p}_p}\right)^{\gamma_{tp}} \left(\frac{p_k}{\bar{p}_k}\right)^{\gamma_{tk}} (\cdots)$$
$$\times \left(\frac{p_b}{\bar{p}_b}\right)^{\gamma_{tb}} \left(\frac{p_c}{\bar{p}_c}\right)^{\gamma_{tc}} \left(\frac{p_d}{\bar{p}_d}\right)^{\gamma_{td}} (\cdots) \left(\frac{i}{\bar{i}}\right)^{\gamma_{ti}}$$
$$\times e^{\gamma'_{tt}\left(\frac{p_t}{\bar{p}_t}-1\right)+\gamma'_{tp}\left(\frac{p_p}{\bar{p}_p}-1\right)+\gamma'_{tk}\left(\frac{p_k}{\bar{p}_k}-1\right)+\cdots+\gamma'_{ti}\left(\frac{i}{\bar{i}}-1\right)},$$ \quad (142)

$$\frac{S_t}{\bar{S}_t} = \left(\frac{p_t}{\bar{p}_t}\right)^{\gamma_{tt}} \left(\frac{p_p}{\bar{p}_p}\right)^{\gamma_{tp}} \left(\frac{p_k}{\bar{p}_k}\right)^{\gamma_{tk}} (\cdots)$$
$$\times \left(\frac{p_b}{\bar{p}_b}\right)^{\gamma_{tb}} \left(\frac{p_c}{\bar{p}_c}\right)^{\gamma_{tc}} \left(\frac{p_d}{\bar{p}_d}\right)^{\gamma_{td}} (\cdots) \left(\frac{i}{\bar{i}}\right)^{\gamma_{ti}}$$
$$\times e^{\gamma'_{tt}\left(\frac{p_t}{\bar{p}_t}-1\right)+\gamma'_{tp}\left(\frac{p_p}{\bar{p}_p}-1\right)+\gamma'_{tk}\left(\frac{p_k}{\bar{p}_k}-1\right)+\cdots+\gamma'_{ti}\left(\frac{i}{\bar{i}}-1\right)}$$
$$\times e^{\frac{1}{2}\left\{\gamma''_{tt}\left[\left(\frac{p_t}{\bar{p}_t}\right)^2-1\right]+\gamma''_{tp}\left[\left(\frac{p_p}{\bar{p}_p}\right)^2-1\right]\right.}$$
$$\left.+\gamma''_{tk}\left[\left(\frac{p_k}{\bar{p}_k}\right)^2-1\right]+\cdots+\gamma''_{ti}\left[\left(\frac{i}{\bar{i}}\right)^2-1\right]\right\}}.$$

The third group contains only one equation, which may take any one of three typical forms the derivation of which we shall explain:

$$\frac{S_\Gamma}{\bar{S}_\Gamma} = \left(\frac{p_t}{\bar{p}_t}\right)^{v\Gamma_t}\left(\frac{p_p}{\bar{p}_p}\right)^{v\Gamma_p}\left(\frac{p_k}{\bar{p}_k}\right)^{v\Gamma_k}(\cdots)$$

$$\times\left(\frac{p_b}{\bar{p}_b}\right)^{v\Gamma_b}\left(\frac{p_c}{\bar{p}_c}\right)^{v\Gamma_c}\left(\frac{p_d}{\bar{p}_d}\right)^{v\Gamma_d}(\cdots)\left(\frac{i}{\bar{i}}\right)^{v\Gamma_i},$$

$$\frac{S_\Gamma}{\bar{S}_\Gamma} = \left(\frac{p_t}{\bar{p}_t}\right)^{v\Gamma_t}\left(\frac{p_p}{\bar{p}_p}\right)^{v\Gamma_p}\left(\frac{p_k}{\bar{p}_k}\right)^{v\Gamma_k}(\cdots)$$

$$\times\left(\frac{p_b}{\bar{p}_b}\right)^{v\Gamma_b}\left(\frac{p_c}{\bar{p}_c}\right)^{v\Gamma_c}\left(\frac{p_d}{\bar{p}_d}\right)^{v\Gamma_d}(\cdots)\left(\frac{i}{\bar{i}}\right)^{v\Gamma_i}$$

$$\times e^{v\Gamma_t'\left(\frac{p_t}{\bar{p}_t}-1\right)+v\Gamma_p'\left(\frac{p_p}{\bar{p}_p}-1\right)+v\Gamma_k'\left(\frac{p_k}{\bar{p}_k}-1\right)+\cdots+v\Gamma_i'\left(\frac{i}{\bar{i}}-1\right)},$$

$$\frac{S_\Gamma}{\bar{S}_\Gamma} = \left(\frac{p_t}{\bar{p}_t}\right)^{v\Gamma_t}\left(\frac{p_p}{\bar{p}_p}\right)^{v\Gamma_p}\left(\frac{p_k}{\bar{p}_k}\right)^{v\Gamma_k}(\cdots)$$

$$\times\left(\frac{p_b}{\bar{p}_b}\right)^{v\Gamma_b}\left(\frac{p_c}{\bar{p}_c}\right)^{v\Gamma_c}\left(\frac{p_d}{\bar{p}_d}\right)^{v\Gamma_d}(\cdots)\left(\frac{i}{\bar{i}}\right)^{v\Gamma_i}$$

$$\times e^{v\Gamma_t'\left(\frac{p_t}{\bar{p}_t}-1\right)+v\Gamma_p'\left(\frac{p_p}{\bar{p}_p}-1\right)+v\Gamma_k'\left(\frac{p_k}{\bar{p}_k}-1\right)+\cdots+v\Gamma_i'\left(\frac{i}{\bar{i}}-1\right)}$$

$$\times e^{\frac{1}{2}\left\{v\Gamma_t''\left[\left(\frac{p_t}{\bar{p}_t}\right)^2-1\right]+v\Gamma_p''\left[\left(\frac{p_p}{\bar{p}_p}\right)^2-1\right]\right.}$$
$$\left._{+v\Gamma_k''\left[\left(\frac{p_k}{\bar{p}_k}\right)^2-1\right]+\cdots+v\Gamma_i''\left[\left(\frac{i}{\bar{i}}\right)^2-1\right]\right\}}.$$

$$(143)$$

These functions descriptive of the supply of credit are derived by the same process as was employed in the deduction of the demand functions for commodities and the supply functions of services. The notions of elasticity and partial elasticity give us the clue to the types of credit functions, and the method of trend-ratios enables us to put the typical functions into forms that may be used in the statistical derivation of the law of supply of credit.

If the function descriptive of the supply of credit is

$$S_\Gamma = F_\Gamma(p_t,\; p_p,\; p_k,\; \cdots p_b,\; p_c,\; p_d,\; \cdots i),$$

the partial elasticity of supply of credit with reference, say, to the rate of interest is

$$s\eta_{\mathrm{r}i\cdot p_t p_p p_k \cdots p_b p_c p_d}\cdots = \frac{\partial S_{\mathrm{r}}}{S_{\mathrm{r}}} \Big/ \frac{\partial i}{i} = \frac{i}{S_{\mathrm{r}}} \cdot \frac{\partial S_{\mathrm{r}}}{\partial i}.$$

Following our procedure in case of demand functions and supply functions, we shall obtain three types of credit functions according as the partial elasticities are given as constants, as linear functions of the corresponding price and interest variables, or as quadratic functions of these variables. Symbolically, this means for the representative variable i,

$$s\eta_{\mathrm{r}i\cdot p_t p_p p_k \cdots p_b p_c p_d}\cdots = \begin{cases} v_{\mathrm{r}i}, \text{ or} \\ v_{\mathrm{r}i} + v'_{\mathrm{r}i}i, \text{ or} \\ v_{\mathrm{r}i} + v'_{\mathrm{r}i}i + v''_{\mathrm{r}i}i^2. \end{cases}$$

Our studies of demand and supply have shown that the three equations given in (143) satisfy, respectively, these three conditions as to the partial elasticities.

The fourth group of equations contributing to the description of the moving general equilibrium contains n equations expressing the equality of the demand for, and the supply of, productive services. Each of these n equations may be expressed in any one of three forms in which the coefficients of production through their constituent factors, partial relative efficiencies of organization, are given as constants, or as linear functions of the respective factors of production, or as quadratic functions of those factors. The three types are:

$$\epsilon_{at}\frac{\overline{p}_a}{\overline{p}_t}D_a + \epsilon_{bt}\frac{\overline{p}_b}{\overline{p}_t}D_b + \epsilon_{ct}\frac{\overline{p}_c}{\overline{p}_t}D_c + \cdots$$

$$+ \epsilon_{kt}\frac{\overline{p}_k}{\overline{p}_t}D_k + \cdots = S_t,$$

$$\left[\epsilon_{at} + \epsilon'_{at}\left(\frac{T_a}{\overline{T}_a}\right)\right]\frac{\overline{p}_a}{\overline{p}_t}D_a$$

$$+ \left[\epsilon_{bt} + \epsilon'_{bt}\left(\frac{T_b}{\overline{T}_b}\right)\right]\frac{\overline{p}_b}{\overline{p}_t}D_b + \cdots$$

$$+ \left[\epsilon_{kt} + \epsilon'_{kt}\left(\frac{T_k}{\overline{T}_k}\right)\right]\frac{\overline{p}_k}{\overline{p}_t}D_k + \cdots = S_t,$$

$$\left[\epsilon_{at} + \epsilon'_{at}\left(\frac{T_a}{\overline{T}_a}\right) + \epsilon''_{at}\left(\frac{T_a}{\overline{T}_a}\right)^2\right]\frac{\overline{p}_a}{\overline{p}_t}D_a$$

$$+ \cdots + \left[\epsilon_{kt} + \epsilon'_{kt}\left(\frac{T_k}{\overline{T}_k}\right)\right.$$

$$\left. + \epsilon''_{kt}\left(\frac{T_k}{\overline{T}_k}\right)^2\right]\frac{\overline{p}_k}{\overline{p}_t}D_k + \cdots = S_t. \tag{144}$$

The fifth group consists of m equations expressing that the prices of the m commodities are equal to their respective costs of production. As the coefficients of production appear in these equations, and as the coefficients themselves may be expressed in the three forms which we have just enumerated, each of the m equations may be given in three ways. The coefficients of production also appear in the sixth group of equations, and, as we shall see, give origin to three types of equations in case of each one of the l capital goods. For a representative commodity (C) in the fifth group, the three typical equations are:

$$\epsilon_{ct}\frac{\bar{p}_c}{\bar{p}_t}p_t + \epsilon_{cp}\frac{\bar{p}_c}{\bar{p}_p}p_p + \epsilon_{ck}\frac{\bar{p}_c}{\bar{p}_k}p_k + \cdots = p_c, \left.\begin{array}{l} \\ \\ \\ \\ \\ \\ \\ \\ \\ \\ \\ \\ \\ \\ \\ \end{array}\right\}$$

$$\left[\epsilon_{ct} + \epsilon'_{ct}\left(\frac{T_c}{\bar{T}_c}\right)\right]\frac{\bar{p}_c}{\bar{p}_t}p_t$$

$$+ \left[\epsilon_{cp} + \epsilon'_{cp}\left(\frac{P_c}{\bar{P}_c}\right)\right]\frac{\bar{p}_c}{\bar{p}_p}p_p$$

$$+ \left[\epsilon_{ck} + \epsilon'_{ck}\left(\frac{K_c}{\bar{K}_c}\right)\right]\frac{\bar{p}_c}{\bar{p}_k}p_k + \cdots = p_c, \quad (145)$$

$$\left[\epsilon_{ct} + \epsilon'_{ct}\left(\frac{T_c}{\bar{T}_c}\right) + \epsilon''_{ct}\left(\frac{T_c}{\bar{T}_c}\right)^2\right]\frac{\bar{p}_c}{\bar{p}_t}p_t$$

$$+ \left[\epsilon_{cp} + \epsilon'_{cp}\left(\frac{P_c}{\bar{P}_c}\right)\right.$$

$$\left. + \epsilon''_{cp}\left(\frac{P_c}{\bar{P}_c}\right)^2\right]\frac{\bar{p}_c}{\bar{p}_p}p_p + \cdots = p_c.$$

The equations of the sixth group express that the prices of the *l* new capital goods are equal to their respective costs of production. For a representative capital good (K), the three typical functions are:

$$\epsilon_{kt}\frac{\bar{p}_k}{\bar{p}_t}p_t + \epsilon_{kp}\frac{\bar{p}_k}{\bar{p}_p}p_p + \epsilon_{kk}\frac{\bar{p}_k}{\bar{p}_k}p_k + \cdots = \Pi_k, \left.\begin{array}{l} \\ \\ \\ \\ \\ \\ \\ \\ \\ \\ \\ \\ \\ \\ \\ \end{array}\right\}$$

$$\left[\epsilon_{kt} + \epsilon'_{kt}\left(\frac{T_k}{\bar{T}_k}\right)\right]\frac{\bar{p}_k}{\bar{p}_t}p_t$$

$$+ \left[\epsilon_{kp} + \epsilon'_{kp}\left(\frac{P_k}{\bar{P}_k}\right)\right]\frac{\bar{p}_k}{\bar{p}_p}p_p + \cdots = \Pi_k, \quad (146)$$

$$\left[\epsilon_{kt} + \epsilon'_{kt}\left(\frac{T_k}{\bar{T}_k}\right) + \epsilon''_{kt}\left(\frac{T_k}{\bar{T}_k}\right)^2\right]\frac{\bar{p}_k}{\bar{p}_t}p_t$$

$$+ \left[\epsilon_{kp} + \epsilon'_{kp}\left(\frac{P_k}{\bar{P}_k}\right) + \epsilon''_{kp}\left(\frac{P_k}{\bar{P}_k}\right)^2\right]$$

$$\times \frac{\bar{p}_k}{\bar{p}_p}p_p + \cdots = \Pi_k.$$

The seventh group consists of only one equation, which expresses the equality of the value of the new capital goods and the supply of credit:

$$D_k \Pi_k + D_{k'} \Pi_{k'} + D_{k''} \Pi_{k''} + \cdots = S_\Gamma. \quad (147)$$

The eighth group contains l equations in which the prices of the capital goods are expressed in terms of the rate of interest and the prices of the services of the respective capital goods:

$$\left. \begin{array}{l} \Pi_k = \dfrac{p_k}{i + \mu_k}, \\[2mm] \Pi_{k'} = \dfrac{p_{k'}}{i + \mu_{k'}}, \\[2mm] \Pi_{k''} = \dfrac{p_{k''}}{i + \mu_{k''}}. \end{array} \right\} \quad (148)$$

These eight groups of equations determining the moving general equilibrium, like the corresponding eight groups in the preceding study on "The Theory of Capitalization," contain in all $(2m + 2n + 2l + 1)$ independent equations. As the number of unknown quantities is likewise $(2m + 2n + 2l + 1)$, the problem of the moving general equilibrium may be solved concretely by means of the preceding laws and technique.

The concrete moving equilibrium which has just been described takes its course along the lines of the general trends of the variables. These general trends in case of the variables of the empirical functions— that is, the demand functions, the supply functions, and the production functions—are the trends obtained from equations fitted to the variables by the method of least squares. In case of the other variables

$$D_k, \Pi_k; \quad D_{k'}, \Pi_{k'}; \quad D_{k''}, \Pi_{k''}; \quad \cdots$$

the general trends are the values of these quantities as they are determined by the ensemble of the equations describing the general equilibrium. The difference in the character of these two kinds of general trends we shall indicate by a separate notation. The general trends obtained by fitting equations to data by the method of least squares we have already indicated by placing a bar over the variables. The general trends of variables determined by the ensemble of the equilibrium equations we shall indicate by placing above the variables two bars. For example, the general trend of D_k is $\bar{\bar{D}}_k$.

We shall now review the eight groups of equations with the purpose of seeing the nature of the moving equilibrium values. In the first group, equations (141), we see that when the prices and the rate of interest have their trend values, the demands for the commodities have their trend values; that is, when every p is equal to the corresponding $\bar{p}$ and i is equal to $\bar{i}$, every D is equal to the corresponding $\bar{D}$. This is true for all three typical equations in (141). Similar results are obtained for the supply equations (142): when every p is equal to the corresponding $\bar{p}$ and i is equal to $\bar{i}$, every S is equal to the corresponding $\bar{S}$. Equation (143) presents a parallel relation: S_r is equal to $\bar{S}_r$ when every p is equal to the corresponding $\bar{p}$ and i is equal to $\bar{i}$. From these three groups of equations, we learn that every D is equal to its trend value, every S is equal to its trend value, and the supply of credit is equal to its trend value when prices and the rate of interest have their trend values. The trend values in these three groups are trend values determined by the method of least squares from empirical data.

The other type of trend values we may most clearly observe by considering the eighth group of equations. When prices and the rate of interest have their empirical trend values, the equations in the group become

$$\overline{\overline{\Pi}}_k = \frac{\overline{p}_k}{\overline{i} + \mu_k},$$

$$\overline{\overline{\Pi}}_{k'} = \frac{\overline{p}_{k'}}{\overline{i} + \mu_{k'}},$$

$$\overline{\overline{\Pi}}_{k''} = \frac{\overline{p}_{k''}}{\overline{i} + \mu_{k''}},$$

. . . .

The remaining four groups of equations contain these two kinds of trend values. In a state of equilibrium, when prices and the rate of interest have their trend values, a typical equation of the fourth group (144) becomes

$$\epsilon_{at}\frac{\overline{p}_a}{\overline{p}_t}\overline{D}_a + \epsilon_{bt}\frac{\overline{p}_b}{\overline{p}_t}\overline{D}_b + \cdots + \epsilon_{kt}\frac{\overline{p}_k}{\overline{p}_t}\overline{\overline{D}}_k + \cdots = \overline{S}_t.$$

A typical equation of the fifth group (145) becomes

$$[\epsilon_{ct} + \epsilon'_{ct}] + [\epsilon_{cp} + \epsilon'_{cp}] + \cdots + [\epsilon_{ck} + \epsilon'_{ck}]$$
$$+ \cdots = 1.$$

A typical equation of the sixth group (146) is

$$[\epsilon_{kt} + \epsilon'_{kt} + \epsilon''_{kt}]\overline{p}_k + [\epsilon_{kp} + \epsilon'_{kp} + \epsilon''_{kp}]\overline{p}_k + \cdots = \overline{\overline{\Pi}}_k.$$

The one equation in (147) becomes

$$\bar{\bar{D}}_k\bar{\bar{\Pi}}_k + \bar{\bar{D}}_{k'}\bar{\bar{\Pi}}_{k'} + \bar{\bar{D}}_{k''}\bar{\bar{\Pi}}_{k''} + \cdots = \bar{S}_r.$$

Statistical Treatment of the Productivity Theory of Distribution

The foregoing theory of a moving general equilibrium affords means of putting to a statistical test the productivity theory of distribution. There are three cardinal features of that doctrine which seem to present insuperable obstacles in the way of statistical verification: (a) The productivity theory obtains only when consumption and production have reached a state of equilibrium. But how may one know when the state of equilibrium is reached? (b) The productivity applies to marginal increments. But how may we isolate the marginal increments? (c) The productivity theory asserts that each factor in production receives an income equal to the number of units of the factor multiplied by its marginal product. But can one prove that the sum of all the several incomes determined by this formula is equal to the product of industry? All three of these difficulties may be removed by the preceding analysis.

(a) The theory of a moving general equilibrium meets the first difficulty. We have shown that the entire economic system oscillates about a general equilibrium moving along the lines of secular trends of prices and products. Trend prices and trend products are equilibrium prices and products.

(b) The empirical derivation of the production function in the form either of (84), (85), (86) or of

(103), (104), (105) meets the second difficulty. If, for example, the production function is of type (104),

$$\frac{Q_c}{\bar{Q}_c} = \left(\frac{T_c}{\bar{T}_c}\right)^{\epsilon_{ct}} \left(\frac{P_c}{\bar{P}_c}\right)^{\epsilon_{cp}} \left(\frac{K_c}{\bar{K}_c}\right)^{\epsilon_{ck}} (\cdots)$$
$$\times e^{\epsilon'_{ct}\left(\frac{T_c}{\bar{T}_c}-1\right)+\epsilon'_{cp}\left(\frac{P_c}{\bar{P}_c}-1\right)+\epsilon'_{ck}\left(\frac{K_c}{\bar{K}_c}-1\right)+\cdots}.$$

then, when the statistical values of the constants in that equation have been determined, the marginal product of any factor may be immediately calculated. For example, the product of ΔT_c would be $(\partial Q_c/\partial T_c)\cdot\Delta T_c$.

(c) A transformation of equations (145) meets the third difficulty.[18] Equations (145) may be written

$$\left.\begin{aligned}
&\left\{\epsilon_{ct}\frac{\bar{p}_c}{\bar{p}_t}\right\}\frac{p_t}{p_c} + \left\{\epsilon_{cp}\frac{\bar{p}_c}{\bar{p}_p}\right\}\frac{p_p}{p_c} \\
&\qquad\qquad + \left\{\epsilon_{ck}\frac{\bar{p}_c}{\bar{p}_k}\right\}\frac{p_k}{p_c} + \cdots = 1, \\[2mm]
&\left\{\left[\epsilon_{rt} + \epsilon'_{ct}\left(\frac{T_c}{\bar{T}_c}\right)\right]\frac{\bar{p}_c}{\bar{p}_t}\right\}\frac{p_t}{p_c} \\
&\qquad + \left\{\left[\epsilon_{cp} + \epsilon'_{cp}\left(\frac{P_c}{\bar{P}_c}\right)\right]\frac{\bar{p}_c}{\bar{p}_p}\right\}\frac{p_p}{p_c} + \cdots = 1, \\[2mm]
&\left\{\left[\epsilon_{ct} + \epsilon'_{ct}\left(\frac{T_c}{\bar{T}_c}\right) + \epsilon''_{ct}\left(\frac{T_c}{\bar{T}_c}\right)^2\right]\frac{\bar{p}_c}{\bar{p}_t}\right\}\frac{p_t}{p_c} \\
&\qquad + \left\{\left[\epsilon_{cp} + \epsilon'_{cp}\left(\frac{P_c}{\bar{P}_c}\right) + \epsilon''_{cp}\left(\frac{P_c}{\bar{P}_c}\right)^2\right]\right. \\
&\qquad\qquad \left.\times\frac{\bar{p}_c}{\bar{p}_p}\right\}\frac{p_p}{p_c} + \cdots = 1.
\end{aligned}\right\} \quad (149)$$

The quantities in the bowed parentheses $\{\cdots\}$ give

[18] Here I make use of a hint given by Walras in his *Note sur la réfutation de la théorie anglaise du fermage de M. Wicksteed* (Lausanne, 1896), pp. 9, 10.

the coefficients of production, respectively, as constants; as linear functions of the quantities of the factors of production; and as quadratic functions of those factors. Since the quantities in the bowed parentheses are coefficients of production, if we multiply the above equations (149) through by Q_c, each one of the equations will become

$$T_c \frac{p_t}{p_c} + P_c \frac{p_p}{p_c} + K_c \frac{p_k}{p_c} + \cdots = Q_c. \qquad (150)$$

Now when the economic system is in a state of equilibrium, the productivity theory is supposed to hold, and we have shown that, when equilibrium is reached, equilibrium prices are trend prices and equilibrium products are trend products. By substituting equilibria values in the above equation (150) we have

$$\overline{T}_c \frac{\overline{p}_t}{\overline{p}_c} + \overline{P}_c \frac{\overline{p}_p}{\overline{p}_c} + \overline{K}_c \frac{\overline{p}_k}{\overline{p}_c} + \cdots = \overline{Q}_c. \qquad (151)$$

Only one more substitution is necessary to prove our point. By availing ourselves of the relations established in (119), the above equation (151) may be written

$$\overline{T}_c \frac{\partial \overline{Q}_c}{\partial \overline{T}_c} + \overline{P}_c \frac{\partial \overline{Q}_c}{\partial \overline{P}_c} + \overline{K}_c \frac{\partial \overline{Q}_c}{\partial \overline{K}_c} + \cdots = \overline{Q}_c, \qquad (152)$$

which is proof, in a form that may be statistically tested, of the proposition that in a state of equilibrium the product of industry is divided according to the productivity formula.

CHAPTER VI

ECONOMIC OSCILLATIONS

"L'état réel est donc celui de continuelles oscillations autour
d'un point central d'équilibre, qui lui-même se déplace."

VILFREDO PARETO

"De même que le lac est parfois profondément troublé par
l'orage, de même aussi le marché est parfois violemment agité
par des crises, qui sont des troubles subits et généraux de l'équilibre. *Et l'on pourrait d'autant mieux réprimer ou prévenir ces
crises qu'on connaîtrait mieux les conditions idéales de l'équilibre.*"

LÉON WALRAS

An economic oscillation may be defined as a complete fluctuation of an economic quantity about its
normal position of equilibrium. The equilibria about
which the oscillations occur are classified in the
chapter on "Fundamental Notions" and are described
in mathematical detail in the preceding chapter on
"Moving Equilibria." The theory of economic equilibria is a prerequisite to an understanding of economic
oscillations. In the present chapter we shall first
inquire into the nature of the interrelation of equilibria
and oscillations in case of particular and of general
moving equilibria and the accompanying oscillations.
We shall then construct an index number of general
prices in which the oscillations of general prices may
be derived by means of some of the elements that enter
into the determination of the moving equilibrium.
Oscillations in general will appear as the results of
perturbations in an economic system striving, under
the influence of relatively static forces, toward a

146

moving general equilibrium. The various sources of perturbations give origin to different types of oscillations, and these several types have been seized upon, in current theories of fluctuations, as approximate explanations of the economic rhythm. A consideration of their joint effect is given in the final section on "A Synthetic Theory of Economic Oscillations."

Oscillations about Particular Equilibria

The phenomenon of oscillation about particular equilibria presents a difficulty that is realized only when one passes from the certainties of pure theory to the probabilities of actual practice. The resolution of the practical difficulty affords, in turn, an experience that puts in a new light the theoretical certainties with which the practical problem is approached. In theoretical economics we are in the habit of taking, as the foundation of our reasoning, the elementary laws of demand and supply, the graphs of which are plane curves that do not change with time. If, for example, the price of a particular commodity is the subject of discussion, the usual approach is to graph the laws of supply and demand by taking as the ordinate the price per unit of commodity, and as the abscissa the quantity of commodity demanded or supplied at the given price. The cutting of the two curves is supposed to determine the "equilibrium price" and the "equilibrium amount." Theories of the measurement of consumer's rent and producer's rent, of the effects of taxation, of plans for increasing the social net benefit are elaborated which rest upon these unchanging demand and supply curves.

The procedure is perfectly justifiable in pure economics, but we do not quite realize the meaning of the theories until we attempt to put them into practice. What, for instance, do we mean by oscillations about a particular equilibrium price? The time-honored answer is this: we mean the fluctuations, in harmony with the laws of supply and demand, about a price that equates demand and supply. We illustrate the meaning by drawing graphs of demand and supply showing how any deviation from the equilibrium amount, or equilibrium price, is followed by oscillations of diminishing amplitude which vanish at the equilibrium quantities. But what right have we to assume that the demand and supply curves remain constant during the period of adjustment? This is a critical question from the point of view of practice, and of synthetic theory which has practice as its goal: it is an impertinence from the point of view of pure, mathematical theory. The mathematical economist might quite justly reply,—"my right to make the assumption is my will to do so." He is concerned with theorems, not with practice, and he inquires, in this particular case, what the effect of perturbation will be on the equilibrium amount, or equilibrium price, *if the curves of demand and supply remain constant.* Logical consistency is his aim, not utility; [1] certainty characterises his conclusions, not probability. His conclusions are

---

[1] *Cf.* Edgeworth: *Mathematical Psychics*, p. 94. "No philosophic objector would maintain that the love of the soul for the universal is then only legitimate, when it has been blessed with the production of the useful. The love of the soul for the universal is undoubtedly capable of extravagance, as in the devotion of Plato to the idea. *Amor ipse ordinate amandus est.* But the limits are to be traced by a loving hand, and not to be narrowed by a too severe construction of utility."

"true" in the sense of being in harmony with his definitions and premises.

The object changes when we pass from pure theory to practice: Utility becomes the goal, and logical consistency is valued in the degree in which it is useful. The pure theorist assumes, when the laws of demand and supply are functions of single variables, that the nature of the demand and supply functions is sufficiently determined by the signs of their first derivatives. If D is the quantity of commodity demanded at price p per unit of commodity, the demand function $D = F(p)$ is for many theoretical purposes sufficiently characterized by the condition

$$F'(p) < 0.$$

If S is the quantity of commodity supplied at price p per unit, the assumption usually made in theoretical work is that the law of supply $S = f(p)$ is characterized by the condition

$$f'(p) > 0.$$

Upon these two assumptions as to the signs of the first derivatives rests the teaching of the classical economists and their modern disciples. But do we know that the conclusions which follow from these assumptions may not be invalidated by the method employed in the concrete derivation of the functions $F(p), f(p)$? Are we at liberty to assume, for example, that we can foretell, in general, the effect of a specific tax upon a commodity whose laws of demand and supply are $F(p)$, $f(p)$ if we do not know how these functions are concretely derived? The difficulty was foreseen by Cournot and put aside, but he dwelt sufficiently long upon the question to state several facts of enormous importance for Synthetic Economics in general and for the theory of oscillations in particular.

Here is Cournot's statement: "To define with accuracy the quantity D, or the function $F(p)$ which is the expression of it, we have supposed that D represented the quantity sold annually throughout the extent of the country or of the market under consideration. In fact, the year is the natural unit of time, especially for researches having any connection with social economy. All the wants of mankind are reproduced during this term, and all the resources which mankind obtains from nature and by labour. Nevertheless, the price of an article may vary notably in the course of a year, and, *strictly speaking, the law of demand may also vary in the same interval, if the country experiences a movement of progress or decadence.* For greater accuracy, therefore, in the expression $F(p)$, p must be held to denote the annual average price, and the curve which represents function F to be itself an average of all the curves which would represent this function at different times of the year. *But this extreme accuracy is only necessary in case it is proposed to go to numerical applications, and it is superfluous for researches which only seek to obtain a general expression of average results, independent of periodic oscillations.*" [2] As usual we are compelled to admire Cournot's penetration into economic realities. This short paragraph gives warn-

[2] Cournot: *Researches into the Mathematical Principles of the Theory of Wealth.* Bacon's translation, pp. 51–52. I have italicized lines important for our purpose.

ing, (a) that the law of demand—and by implication also the law of supply—may vary "if the country experiences a movement of progress or decadence"; (b) that the type of mathematical theory represented by Cournot gives only "a general expression of average results"; (c) that when we go on to numerical applications, cognizance must be taken of the variations of the empirical demand and supply functions.

As to the theory of oscillations about particular equilibria, Cournot makes clear that we shall have to take account not only of the oscillations that may theoretically occur about a stable equilibrium when the demand and supply functions are constant, but also of the oscillations that actually take place about moving equilibria when the demand and supply functions themselves are in process of change. The methods described in foregoing chapters for determining empirically the laws of demand and supply are adapted to show any variation that may occur with the progress of time in the nature of these functions.

Inasmuch as Synthetic Economics comprises both the rational and the empirical branches of economic science, Cournot's warnings concerning the demand functions apply to every empirical function that figures in the system of equations determining the moving equilibrium. All of these empirical functions are average functions, and the averages vary with the passing of time. Moreover, there are short-time, intermediate-time, and long-time variations, the nature of which the methods of deriving the functions are competent to disclose.

The Mechanism of Oscillations about General Equilibria

Just as Cournot's statical theory of particular equilibria is the point of departure for a concrete, dynamic theory of oscillations about particular equilibria, so Walras' statical theory of general equilibria is the point of departure for a concrete, dynamic theory of oscillations about general equilibria. Availing himself of a hint given by Cournot,[3] Walras [4] has shown how perturbations of a general equilibrium are diffused throughout the whole economic system, setting up oscillations which, with the flow of time, progressively diminish in amplitude until they are extinguished and equilibrium is restored. Walras' scheme, like Cournot's, is purely abstract and his procedure, like Cournot's, raises the question of the legitimacy of the implied assumption that the empirical functions remain constant during the period of perturbation and adjustment.

The answer to the question in case of particular equilibria we found in the nature of the method employed in the derivation of the empirical laws of demand and supply. These empirical laws may be obtained in a way that takes cognizance of the changes in their form with the passing of time. The method of their derivation enables us to arrive not only at average forms of these functions for any desired period of time, but also, if need be, at variants about their average forms. When account is taken of

[3] Cournot: *Researches*, § 76, p. 131, particularly the statement ". . . the general principles of analysis will show us that they must go on with gradually decreasing amplitude."

[4] Walras: *Éléments d'économie politique pure.* Quatrième édition, 25me Leçon, pp. 261–274.

this method of deriving the empirical functions of demand and supply we may pass with safety to a theory of concrete oscillations about a moving, real, particular equilibrium.

A similar course of reasoning holds with reference to a theory of oscillations about general equilibria. The statical, hypothetical limitations of Walras' construction are removed by the method of deriving the empirical functions that enter into the system of equations determining the general equilibrium. These empirical functions are of four kinds:

(a) The laws of demand for commodities;

(b) The laws of supply of services;

(c) The law of supply of credit;

(d) The coefficients of production.

In the preceding chapters we have shown that all four of these groups of empirical functions may be concretely, dynamically determined with any degree of flexibility required by actual practice. Their determination, it is true, leads to forms of functions representing average values, but, if need be, variants about the average forms may be obtained by the same method of derivation. When these concrete, dynamic functions are substituted in Walras' reasoning for his hypothetical, static functions, the new system of equations, as we saw in the preceding chapter, determines a moving equilibrium, and Walras' analysis of oscillations about a static general equilibrium becomes available for a description of concrete oscillations about a moving, real, general equilibrium.

An Index Number of the Oscillations of General Prices

Pantaleoni, in one of his last contributions to political economy, called attention to a problem in the theory of prices the solution of which he regarded as essential to successful practical forecasting. Discussing an alien theme, he observed, incidentally, that the idea of elasticity of demand is one of the most fertile for the progress of economics, but that it is far, even today, from being completely exploited. He then offered a stimulating suggestion:

"The field in which the idea of elasticity of demand is not exploited is this: the correlation of prices of distinct commodities is a function of the elasticities of their curves of demand: if one price varies, the correlations of the other prices will vary according to the elasticity of the demand of the commodity that initiates the change: until this field is adequately explored it will not be possible to have an economic semiology." [5]

The method of the preceding chapters will enable us not only to make a first clearing in this promising field but also to appropriate its yield to the development of the theory of oscillations.

[5] "Con la concezione della rendita del consumatore era data anche quella della elasticità delle curve di domanda e di offerta, idea questa delle più feconde per l'ulteriore progresso della nostra scienza e lungi, anche oggi, dall'essere stata intieramente sfruttata."

"Il campo in cui essa non è sfruttata è questo: la correlazione dei prezzi di merci distinte è una funzione dalla elasticità delle loro curve ai vari prezzi di cui le curve sono il locus. Le correlazioni mutano assai radicalmente se varia un prezzo, a seconda della variazione dell'elasticità della curva della merce il cui prezzo è variato. Non sarà possibile una semiotica economica prima che questo campo non sia stato adeguatamente perlustrato."

Giornale degli Economisti, Gennaio-Febbraio (1924), p. 3, 3n.

Pantaleoni's problem relates to elasticity of demand, which has been designated by η and defined as the ratio of the relative change in the quantity of commodity demanded to the relative change in the price per unit of commodity; that is to say,

$$\eta = \frac{dD}{D} \bigg/ \frac{dp}{p} = \frac{p}{D} \cdot \frac{dD}{dp}. \quad \text{Chapter III, equation (5)}$$

The similar quantity, flexibility of price, denoted by ϕ, has been defined as the ratio of the relative change in the price per unit of the commodity to the relative change in the quantity of the commodity demanded. That is to say,

$$\phi = \frac{dp}{p} \bigg/ \frac{dD}{D} = \frac{D}{p} \cdot \frac{dp}{dD}. \quad \text{Chapter III, equation (6)}$$

Useful and simple demand functions have been derived from these definitions of ϕ and η by placing

$$\phi = \begin{cases} \alpha, \text{ or} \\ \alpha + \alpha'D, \text{ or} \\ \alpha + \alpha'D + \alpha''D^2 \end{cases}$$

or by placing

$$\eta = \begin{cases} \beta, \text{ or} \\ \beta + \beta'p, \text{ or} \\ \beta + \beta'p + \beta''p^2. \end{cases}$$

The simple demand functions derived from the above differential equations are obtained on the assumption either that the price of the commodity is a function only of the quantity of commodity demanded, or that the quantity of commodity demanded is a function of its own price alone. But it is common knowledge that the price of a particular commodity is a function not only of the quantity of the particular commodity in question, but also of the quantities of all other commodities that are demanded. The same idea is conveyed in another way by saying that the quantity of any one commodity demanded is a function not only of its own price but of the prices of all other commodities. To pass from the simple demand functions to accurate descriptions of the real *consensus* [6] of the factors, cognizance must be taken of the complex interrelations of all quantities and all prices.

This transition we have effected by developing the conceptions of elasticity and flexibility. Corresponding to the simple ideas of flexibility of prices and elasticity of demand there are the kindred ideas of partial flexibility of prices and partial elasticity of demand. Suppose that there are n commodities whose quantities and prices are interrelated, and that the price trend-ratios are represented by $p_1/\bar{p}_1, \cdots p_n/\bar{p}_n$, and the quantity-of-commodity trend-ratios by $D_1/\bar{D}_1$, $\cdots D_n/\bar{D}_n$. The functional relations of the variables may be described by taking either the p's or the D's as

[6] "We can never either understand in theory or command in practice the condition of a society in any one respect, without taking into consideration its condition in all other respects. There is no social phenomenon which is not more or less influenced by every other part of the condition of the same society, and therefore by every cause which is influencing any other of the contemporaneous social phenomena. There is, in short, what physiologists term a *consensus*, similar to that existing among the various organs and functions of the physical frame of man and the more perfect animals." J. S. Mill: *A System of Logic*, Bk. VI, Chap. IX, section 2.

the independent variables. If the independent variables are assumed to be the D's, the functions are

$$\frac{p_1}{\bar{p}_1} = f_1\left(\frac{D_1}{\bar{D}_1}, \; \cdots \; \frac{D_q}{\bar{D}_q}, \; \cdots \; \frac{D_n}{\bar{D}_n}\right),$$

$$\frac{p_2}{\bar{p}_2} = f_2\left(\frac{D_1}{\bar{D}_1}, \; \cdots \; \frac{D_q}{\bar{D}_q}, \; \cdots \; \frac{D_n}{\bar{D}_n}\right),$$

$$\cdots \cdots \cdots \cdots \cdots$$

$$\frac{p_n}{\bar{p}_n} = f_n\left(\frac{D_1}{\bar{D}_1}, \; \cdots \; \frac{D_q}{\bar{D}_q}, \; \cdots \; \frac{D_n}{\bar{D}_n}\right).$$

When the simple demand function was assumed to be

$$\frac{p}{\bar{p}} = f\left(\frac{D}{\bar{D}}\right),$$

the flexibility of prices was defined as

$$\phi = \frac{D}{p} \cdot \frac{dp}{dD}.$$

If, now, the more complex dependence of price upon quantities of commodities is taken in the form of the above equations, the partial flexibilities of prices for the representative price p_q will be (Chapter III, equation 32)

$$\phi_{qD_1 \cdot D_2 D_3 \cdots D_n} = \frac{D_1}{p_q} \cdot \frac{\partial p_q}{\partial D_1},$$

$$\cdots \cdots \cdots \cdots$$

$$\phi_{qD_n \cdot D_1 D_2 \cdots D_{n-1}} = \frac{D_n}{p_q} \cdot \frac{\partial p_q}{\partial D_n}.$$

In the chapter on "The Law of Demand" we found,

where price is a function of the quantities of all commodities, useful forms of the function may be obtained by assuming the partial flexibilities of price to be equal to constants, or to vary as linear functions of the quantities of commodity, or to vary as quadratic functions of the quantities of commodity (Chapter III, equation 32). For the price p_q of a representative commodity (Q), the symbolic expression of these three hypotheses with respect to D_1 would be

$$\phi_{qD_1 \cdot D_2 D_3 \cdots D_n} = \frac{D_1}{p_q} \cdot \frac{\partial p_q}{\partial D_1} = \begin{cases} \alpha_{q1}, \text{ or} \\ \alpha_{q1} + \alpha'_{q1} D_1, \text{ or} \\ \alpha_{q1} + \alpha'_{q1} D_1 + \alpha''_{q1} D_1^2. \end{cases}$$

The demand functions satisfying the three hypotheses are, respectively (Chapter III, equations 33, 34, 35),

$$\frac{p_q}{\bar{p}_q} = Constant \left(\frac{D_1}{\bar{D}_1}\right)^{\alpha_{q1}} \left(\frac{D_2}{\bar{D}_2}\right)^{\alpha_{q2}} \left(\cdots\right) \left(\frac{D_n}{\bar{D}_n}\right)^{\alpha_{qn}}; \quad (153)$$

$$\frac{p_q}{\bar{p}_q} = Constant \left(\frac{D_1}{\bar{D}_1}\right)^{\alpha_{q1}} \left(\frac{D_2}{\bar{D}_2}\right)^{\alpha_{q2}} \left(\cdots\right) \left(\frac{D_n}{\bar{D}_n}\right)^{\alpha_{qn}}$$
$$\times e^{\alpha'_{q1}\left(\frac{D_1}{\bar{D}_1}\right) + \alpha'_{q2}\left(\frac{D_2}{\bar{D}_2}\right) + \cdots + \alpha'_{qn}\left(\frac{D_n}{\bar{D}_n}\right)}; \quad (154)$$

$$\frac{p_q}{\bar{p}_q} = Constant \left(\frac{D_1}{\bar{D}_1}\right)^{\alpha_{q1}} \left(\frac{D_2}{\bar{D}_2}\right)^{\alpha_{q2}} \left(\cdots\right) \left(\frac{D_n}{\bar{D}_n}\right)^{\alpha_{qn}}$$
$$\times e^{\alpha'_{q1}\left(\frac{D_1}{\bar{D}_1}\right) + \alpha'_{q2}\left(\frac{D_2}{\bar{D}_2}\right) + \cdots + \alpha'_{qn}\left(\frac{D_n}{\bar{D}_n}\right)}$$
$$\times e^{\frac{1}{2}\left\{\alpha''_{q1}\left(\frac{D_1}{\bar{D}_1}\right)^2 + \alpha''_{q2}\left(\frac{D_2}{\bar{D}_2}\right)^2 + \cdots + \alpha''_{qn}\left(\frac{D_n}{\bar{D}_n}\right)^2\right\}}. \quad (155)$$

Index numbers of price oscillations which will reproduce the empirical data with increasing accuracy may be constructed from equations 153, 154, 155. Let us begin with equation 153, which may be put in the form

$$\log\left(\frac{p_q}{\bar{p}_q}\right) = Constant + \alpha_{q1}\log\left(\frac{D_1}{\bar{D}_1}\right)$$
$$+ \alpha_{q2}\log\left(\frac{D_2}{\bar{D}_2}\right) + \cdots + \alpha_{qn}\log\left(\frac{D_n}{\bar{D}_n}\right). \quad (156)$$

Since this equation is a linear function of the α-coefficients, there is no technical difficulty in fitting it to the observations by the method of least squares. If the fitting were actually carried out and the α-coefficients were statistically determined, the typical function (156) would give the most probable value of $\log(p_q/\bar{p}_q)$ when account had been taken of the dependence of p_q not only upon the oscillation of D_q, but also upon the oscillations in the actual sales of all other commodities.

Theoretically it would be possible to evaluate similar demand functions for all the remaining $(n-1)$ commodities. If such an exhaustive statistical research were carried out, the results would yield n demand functions in which the price of each of the commodities would be given in form (156), where the most probable logarithm of each price oscillation is given as a function of the logarithms of the respective quantity-of-commodity oscillations.

An index number of the most probable price oscillations could be derived, obviously, from these n equations in form (156) giving the probable oscillations of the respective n individual prices. If I were put for the index number, its formula would be

$$n \log I = \log \left(\frac{p_1}{\bar{p}_1} \right) + \log \left(\frac{p_2}{\bar{p}_2} \right)$$
$$+ \cdots + \log \left(\frac{p_n}{\bar{p}_n} \right). \quad (157)$$

By substituting for the logarithms in (157) the corresponding values given in (156) and then summing, we would obtain as a final result [7]

$$n \log I = Constant + \log \left(\frac{D_1}{\bar{D}_1} \right) \Sigma \alpha_1$$
$$+ \log \left(\frac{D_2}{\bar{D}_2} \right) \Sigma \alpha_2 + \cdots + \log \left(\frac{D_n}{\bar{D}_n} \right) \Sigma \alpha_n. \quad (158)$$

Equation (158) expresses a very important economic relation. It gives the oscillations of probable prices in terms of partial flexibilities of prices. The logarithm of the index number of probable price oscillations is a linear function of the respective sums of the partial flexibilities of prices.

We may stop for a moment to consider the bearing upon Pantaleoni's problem of the preceding argument. Pantaleoni stated his semiological problem in these words:

"The field in which the idea of elasticity of demand is not exploited is this: The correlation of prices of distinct commodities is a function of the elasticities of their curves of demand: if one price varies, the correla-

---

[7] If it should be desired to take account of the question of weights, which is ignored in the above argument, there are several well-known devices by means of which that could be done.

tions of the other prices will vary according to the elasticity of demand of the commodity that initiates the change: until this field is adequately explored it will not be possible to have an economic semiology."

Toward the exploration of this virginal field the foregoing discussion makes these contributions:

(i) A first approximation to the general demand function may be taken in the form (156), which is

$$\log \left(\frac{p_q}{\bar{p}_q} \right) = Constant + \alpha_{q1} \log \left(\frac{D_1}{\bar{D}_1} \right)$$
$$+ \alpha_{q2} \log \left(\frac{D_2}{\bar{D}_2} \right) + \cdots + \alpha_{qn} \left(\frac{D_n}{\bar{D}_n} \right),$$

where p_q is the price per unit of representative commodity (Q); $\bar{p}_q$ is the trend of the price per unit of (Q); α_{q1} is the partial flexibility of price p_q with respect to quantity of commodity D_1.

(ii) If the above equation (156) is taken to represent the general demand function, a slightly different wording from that given by Pantaleoni will express the real relations of the quantities in a way that may be empirically tested. According to (156) the following relations are evident:

(a) The logarithmic oscillation of the price of any commodity is a linear function of the partial flexibilities of the given price oscillations with respect to the commodity oscillations;

(b) As a first approximation, it is true that the
variation in a price oscillation is according
to the partial flexibility of the given price
with respect to the commodity that initiates the change. For example, the varia-
tion in log $(p_q/\bar{p}_q)$ is according to α_{q1} if
$(D_1/\bar{D}_1)$ initiates the change.

(iii) Since the α-coefficients in (156) are simple
"regressions" in logarithmic "regression equations," it is possible to resolve them into correlation coefficients and standard deviations.
Such a resolution in case of (156) would display
the interrelations of the factors whose combi-
nations make up the partial flexibilities of
prices.

(iv) An index number of oscillations of general
prices may be constructed from the individual
price oscillations expressed in form (156).
Such an index number is given in (158). The
general proposition formulated in (158) is this:
The logarithm of the index number of price
oscillations is a linear function of the respective
sums of the partial flexibilities of prices.

We have said that a more accurate index number of
price oscillations could be obtained by starting with the
general demand function in form (154) instead of (153).
If the start were made with the demand function of
form (154), then, by an argument in all points similar
to that which was employed when the demand function was of form (153), we should reach an index num-

ber of price oscillations which would be expressed as follows:

$$n \log I = Constant + \log\left(\frac{D_1}{\overline{D}_1}\right)\Sigma\alpha_1$$

$$+ \log\left(\frac{D_2}{\overline{D}_2}\right)\Sigma\alpha_2 + \cdots + \log\left(\frac{D_n}{\overline{D}_n}\right)\Sigma\alpha_n$$

$$+ \left[\frac{D_1}{\overline{D}_1}\Sigma\alpha_1' + \frac{D_2}{\overline{D}_2}\Sigma\alpha_2' + \cdots \right.$$

$$\left. + \frac{D_n}{\overline{D}_n}\Sigma\alpha_n'\right]\log e. \tag{159}$$

A Synthetic Theory of Economic Oscillations

The advantages of the synthetic method in economic research were briefly referred to in the "Introduction." The statement was made that the synthetic method of treating as an ensemble the totality of prices and their determinants eliminates many controversies in economics; it enables the investigator to know when his problem has reached a solution; and it gives ground for the hope of introducing into economic life rational forecasting and control. These advantages have been shown in detail in the theory of "Moving Equilibria" and will be still further exemplified in a synthetic theory of economic oscillations.

First, with regard to the elimination of controversies. In the contemporary investigation of oscillations we are passing through exactly the same throes of research as characterized the long, difficult endeavor after clearness, accuracy, and reality in the treatment of other economic problems, as, for example, the causes of value, the causes of the rate of wages, and the causes of the rate of interest. Each of these questions has many aspects; each aspect supplies material for a novel description; and every new description is held as exclusively veracious by the happy describer and his partisans. But in case of these older problems the preceding chapter on "Moving Equilibria" has shown that most theories of value, wages, and interest contain a partial truth; that the sum of the partial truths is not the whole truth; that the relative place and weight of each truth may be specified; and that the ensemble of determining conditions may be mathematically expressed. Similar statements may be made with regard to theories as to the causes of economic oscillations.

Secondly, let us observe that an essential characteristic of the synthetic method is that it enables the investigator to know when his problem has reached a solution. The criterion of solution in synthetic economics is the same as the criterion in synthetic chemistry, viz., the synthetic reproduction of a compound from previously analysed original elements. The act of synthesizing implies knowledge, qualitative and quantitative, not only of the original constituent elements but also of the mechanism and the process of synthesis. In economics the analogue is quite a different thing from a philosophic, eclectic recognition of the grain of truth in all things erroneous, which, from the point of view of the synthetic method with action and control as its goal, is simply practical impotence.

An economic oscillation we have defined as a complete fluctuation of an economic quantity about its normal position of equilibrium. The synthetic theory of oscillations presupposes a knowledge of the synthetic theory of general equilibria, not only because the latter theory relates to the normals about which the oscillations occur, but because it supplies a description of the economic mechanism which functions as an ensemble of parts in a state of continuous oscillations about positions of moving equilibria. The ties between the parts of the ensemble, which in the economic ensemble are expressed by mathematical equations, determine the nature of the related oscillatory motions of the parts.

Progress in the description of this oscillatory ensemble is made by two types of successive approximations, which we may call, respectively, successive approximations in solidarity of data and successive approximations in accuracy of mathematical formulas. These methodological devices are abundantly illustrated in the preceding chapter. The increasing solidarity has reference to the enlarging range of data brought into relations of interdependence; the successive approximations in mathematical accuracy refer to the degrees of fidelity in the mathematical descriptions of the relations of mutual dependence. The solidarity of the economic system is regarded, first, simply from the point of view of the exchange of consumable goods and services: the problem consists in determining the quantities of goods and services exchanged and the rates at which the exchanges are made; no account is taken of the problems of production, capitalization, or distribution. By increasing approximation in solidarity all of these phases of the economic process are shown to be interdependent, and no one aspect of economic activity may be understood without reference to all the rest. The successive approximations in the mathematical descriptions of the interrelations of the phenomena are generally, but not always, achieved by the use of increasingly complex functions. The parameters of the functions are assumed, at first, to be constants and are then allowed to vary according to convenient formulas.

These two processes—the process of successive approximations in solidarity and the process of successive approximations in accuracy—which together characterize in the degree of their completeness the measure of the progress of the science, make possible the apprehension of the origin and nature of oscillations. Increasing approximation in solidarity implies the necessity for prolonging the *time* over which the economic synthesis must extend, and *time*, as Marshall said, "is the centre of the chief difficulties of almost every economic problem": [8] it involves exposure to contingencies, growth or decay; inevitable errors in forecasts; and unavoidable lags and leads in adjustments. Successive approximations in the mathematical formulation become both more difficult and more hazardous because of the enlarging scope of the data, the multiplicity of interrelations, and the increasing complexity of the individual mathematical functions. But the larger synthesis, with its mathematical, quasi-mechanical description of the industrial organism, reveals in its fidelity and completeness the critical, sensitive spots of the organism. These

[8] Marshall: *Principles of Economics*, 4th edit., p. x.

sensitive spots are the sources of the oscillations the nature of which is apprehended through the mathematical description of the mechanical functioning of the organism.

The description of moving equilibria in the preceding chapter was given in a first and a second approximation. In the second, and more complete approximation, eight groups of equations were described whose co-existence determines the moving equilibrium. We shall review these eight groups for the purpose of pointing out the sensitive spots in which the oscillations have their origin. The system of equations will also show the mechanism through which, as we have seen in a previous section, a perturbation in any sensitive spot will diffuse throughout the organism an oscillatory motion. We shall find that the perturbations in certain spots are cumulative in effects, and in others are non-cumulative; that in certain spots perturbations are recurrent, while in others they are non-recurrent. A simple classification of perturbations would, therefore, be

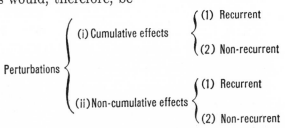

The first three groups of the eight whose co-existence determines the moving general equilibrium are made up of empirical functions of demand for commodities, empirical functions of supply of services, and the

empirical function of supply of credit. Representative functions in these groups are the function of demand for commodity (C),

$$\frac{D_c}{\overline{D}_c} = F_c\left(\frac{p_t}{\overline{p}_t}, \frac{p_p}{\overline{p}_p}, \frac{p_k}{\overline{p}_k}, \cdots \frac{p_b}{\overline{p}_b}, \frac{p_c}{\overline{p}_c}, \frac{p_d}{\overline{p}_d}, \cdots \frac{i}{\overline{i}}\right);$$

the function of supply of service (T),

$$\frac{S_t}{\overline{S}_t} = F_t\left(\frac{p_t}{\overline{p}_t}, \frac{p_p}{\overline{p}_p}, \frac{p_k}{\overline{p}_k}, \cdots \frac{p_b}{\overline{p}_b}, \frac{p_c}{\overline{p}_c}, \frac{p_d}{\overline{p}_d}, \cdots \frac{i}{\overline{i}}\right);$$

the function of supply of credit (Γ),

$$\frac{S_\Gamma}{\overline{S}_\Gamma} = F_\Gamma\left(\frac{p_t}{\overline{p}_t}, \frac{p_p}{\overline{p}_p}, \frac{p_k}{\overline{p}_k}, \cdots \frac{p_b}{\overline{p}_b}, \frac{p_c}{\overline{p}_c}, \frac{p_d}{\overline{p}_d}, \cdots \frac{i}{\overline{i}}\right).$$

Before passing on to recall the other groups of equations, we may illustrate with these three groups the meaning of the above classification of perturbations and the significance of the term, sensitive spot. All three of the above representative equations are functions of three classes of independent variables: (1) prices of services, p_t, p_p, p_k, $\cdots$; (2) prices of commodities, p_b, p_c, p_d, $\cdots$; and (3) the price of credit, namely, the rate of interest i. Moreover, all of the prices of the various services and commodities are in terms of the standard of value, which is assumed to be commodity (A). Now it is quite clear that a perturbation of prices having its origin in the standard of value (A) would be cumulative in its effects inasmuch as it would, with varying degrees of promptness, affect in the same direction all prices, which in turn would entail an oscillatory readjustment of the whole economic system. (Here is the truth upon which rest those incomplete theories of oscillations which depend for their explanation upon variations in the quantity of money.) On the other hand, a perturbation in the price of (C) would affect in different ways the prices of other commodities, causing some to rise in price, others, to fall. There would be no general movement of prices in the same direction and no need of readjustment of the whole economic system. The perturbation in the standard of value is cumulative in its effects, while the perturbation in the price of the consumer's good (C) is non-cumulative. The medium of exchange is a sensitive spot in the economic organism.

The first group of prices among the independent variables in the above empirical functions refer to the prices of services. Let us consider the service of land (T). Suppose, that in consequence of fluctuations in the weather, the price of the service of land per unit of commodity produced is in a state of constant oscillation. Since the price of the service of land is a factor in the cost of all food products and many raw materials of manufactures, perturbations in the price of (T) are cumulative in their effects; and since the fluctuations in the weather are recurrent, the perturbations in the price of (T) are cumulative in effects and recurrent. The prices (p_t, p_p, p_k, $\cdots$) among the independent variables constitute a sensitive spot in the economic organism.

Another point should be noted before we leave these empirical functions. All of the functions of which D_c, S_t, S_r are representative are average functions. They are the mean results of synchronous variations of prices and quantities demanded and supplied over a constantly varying period of time. The variation of these functions from their respective mean values will produce oscillations. This is particularly true of the function of supply of credit S_r, for the reason that the supply function of credit fluctuates between wide limits; the fluctuation is cumulative in its effects and is recurrent. (Those theories of the trade, or business, cycle which rest for their explanation upon oscillations between errors of optimism and errors of pessimism on the part of the business world have, in the variation of the empirical functions, a foundation for the partial truth they contain.)

The fourth, fifth, and sixth groups of equations introduce coefficients of production, which constitute another sensitive spot in the economic organism.

The fourth group of equations expresses the equality of the demand for productive services and their supply. One of the representative equations given in (144) may be expressed in the form,

$$\left\{ \left[\epsilon_{at} + \epsilon'_{at}\left(\frac{T_a}{\overline{T}_a} \right) \right] \frac{\bar{p}_a}{\bar{p}_t} \right\} D_a + \cdots = S_t. \quad (160)$$

The fifth group expresses the equality of the prices of consumers' goods and their respective costs. One of the representative equations in (145) may be put in the form,

$$\left\{ \left[\epsilon_{ct} + \epsilon'_{ct}\left(\frac{T_c}{\overline{T}_c} \right) \right] \frac{\bar{p}_c}{\bar{p}_t} \right\} p_t + \cdots = p_c. \quad (161)$$

The sixth group expresses the equality of the prices of the producers' goods and their costs of production.

One of the representative equations in (146) may be written

$$\left\{\left[\epsilon_{kt} + \epsilon_{kt}'\left(\frac{T_k}{\overline{T}_k}\right)\right]\frac{\overline{p}_k}{\overline{p}_t}\right\}p_t + \cdots = \Pi_k. \quad (162)$$

In all three of these groups the quantities in the bowed parentheses $\{\cdots\}$ are the coefficients of production.

Equation (160) rests upon the hypothesis that in a state of equilibrium the demand for a productive service is equal to its supply. The items making up the demand are specified on the left-hand side of the equation; the supply is given by the empirical supply function,

$$\frac{S_t}{\overline{S}_t} = F_t\left(\frac{p_t}{\overline{p}_t}, \frac{p_p}{\overline{p}_p}, \frac{p_k}{\overline{p}_k}, \cdots \frac{p_b}{\overline{p}_b}, \frac{p_c}{\overline{p}_c}, \frac{p_d}{\overline{p}_d}, \cdots \frac{i}{\overline{i}}\right).$$

This explicit statement of the items on both sides of the equation enables us to see the conditions under which demand and supply diverge from equality, and we know, from the second section of this chapter, that every divergence in demand and supply sets up an oscillation of readjustment.

Equations (161) and (162) rest upon the hypothesis that in a state of equilibrium the prices of consumers' goods and producers' goods are equal to their respective costs of production. The items constituting the costs are specified on the left-hand side of the equation, so that it is possible to see how oscillations may have their origin here in the divergence of cost and price.

All three of the equations (160), (161), (162) contain the coefficients of production, which are given in the bowed parentheses, and these coefficients, as we have said, are sensitive spots in the organism.   This is true for a double reason: any change in the coefficients of production affects not only the prices of both consumers' and producers' goods, but also the incomes of all factors in production.   The last section of the preceding chapter, dealing with the "Statistical Treatment of the Productivity Theory of Distribution," showed how variations in the coefficients of production are followed by variations in the distribution of the product of industry.   The lag in the adjustment of income to the varying coefficients of production is a prolific source of cumulative, recurrent oscillations. (Here is the basis of truth in theories that trace business fluctuations to "mal-adjustment of income.")

The seventh and eighth groups of equations contributing to the description of the moving equilibrium reveal the sensitive spot which is particularly associated with the making of producers' goods and the determination of the rate of interest.   The seventh group contains only one equation (147), namely

$$D_k\Pi_k + D_{k'}\Pi_{k'} + D_{k''}\Pi_{k''} + \cdots = S_{\mathrm{r}}. \quad (163)$$

A representative equation of the eighth group (148) is

$$\Pi_k = \frac{p_k}{i + \mu_k}. \quad (164)$$

Equation (163) asserts that the value of the new capital goods is equal to the amount of credit, which, in a state of equilibrium, is equal to the amount of savings.   Equation (164) expresses the fact that, in a state of equilibrium, the price of a capital good (K) is equal to the earnings of such a good divided by the sum of the rate of interest and the rate of insurance and amortisation.

With regard to these relations it is particularly true that *time* is the source of the chief difficulties. Neither (163) nor (164) is true except in a state of equilibrium, and *time* is needed to bring about equilibrium when savings are made, new capital goods are manufactured, and the rate of interest is adjusted to the earnings of capital goods. The delay in adjustment is cumulative and recurrent in its effects. Moreover, while it is true that in a state of equilibrium the value of the new capital goods is equal to the volume of credit, and the volume of credit is equal to the amount of savings, it is also true that at no other time is the volume of credit identical with savings. The divergence of the two is cumulative and recurrent in its effects. (Here, in these cumulative, recurrent phenomena, is the fund of truth in all those theories of economic "cycles" that emphasize the capitalistic or roundabout process of production, the excessive accumulation of capital equipment, and the lag in the adjustment of the rate of interest.)

The preceding review of the sensitive spots in the economic organism, with the revelation of the sources of perturbation of general equilibria and the description of the mechanism of the oscillatory diffusion throughout the economic system of cumulative perturbations, has given an opportunity to point out the partial truth in the leading contemporary theories of trade oscillations. The sum of the partial truths does not constitute the whole truth. To approximate that goal it is necessary to estimate the relative importances of the several truths and to show how the imputed relative importances are integrated into an approximation of the whole truth. The analysis must be justified by an ultimate synthesis.

The investigations of this chapter seem to warrant the statement that the theory of moving equilibria gives a synthetic view of all sources of oscillations, and that it affords a technique, not only for appraising the relative importance of perturbations in the various sensitive spots of the industrial organism, but also for giving the oscillatory resultant of simultaneous perturbations in any number of sensitive spots. If these conclusions are warranted, we may properly speak of a synthetic theory of economic oscillations.

CHAPTER VII

CONCLUSION

"Nos autem ea quae sunt in usu vitaque communi, non ea quae finguntur aut optantur, spectare debemus."

CICERO

The economist is like a scion of a noble race who is proud of his honorable descent and not a little ashamed of his own scant achievements. He cannot fail to have pleasure in Cicero's grouping economic forecasting with astronomic forecasting, and his pride of ancestry is gratified when he is told that both arts were practiced by the father of Greek speculation.[1] The story is well known how Thales of Miletus collected from Babylonian sources statistical data bearing upon the eclipse of the sun, and then predicted by mathematical methods a solar eclipse which actually took place in the reign of Astyages. The discovery of the regularity of cosmical phenomena and the possibility of foreseeing their occurrence was the beginning of a secular movement which Socrates vainly sought to stay: It foretold the death of the gods!

The story of Thales' adventure into economic forecasting has had a history which is singularly connected with the discovery of regularity in human affairs and the use of mathematical methods in forecasting human conduct. The variant of the story as told by Aristotle[2] is that Thales, knowing from his astronomic

---

[1] Cicero: *De Divinatione*, I, xlix.

[2] Aristotle: *Politics*, Bk. I, chap. xi.

175

studies that the crop of olives would be unusually large, bought up the control of the oil presses in Miletus and Chios and, when the crop came to be harvested, he let out the presses at monopoly rates. He was led into this business venture, according to Aristotle, not by the desire for wealth but to prove to those who reviled lovers of wisdom that it was easy for philosophers to make money if they chose to do so. The tale is used by Aristotle to illustrate how the art of making money (χρηματιστική) is quite a different thing from the art of increasing natural wealth (οἰκονομική). The distinction is essentially the same as a very recent one between "business economics" and "welfare economics."

Aristotle's distinction between chrematistics and economics has been exploited consciously and systematically by the mathematical economists. The art of using mathematical methods in the service of science consists in seizing upon those parts of the subject matter that are both critical in importance and quantitative in character, and then discovering relations between these immediately measurable, and other less obviously quantitative, facts. The test of the sufficiency of the mathematical *liaison* in each individual case is its rendering possible the forecasting of the unknown from the relation with the known. An index of the state of perfection of the science is the degree in which these mathematical connections are extended over the range of the subject matter of the science. The genius of Cournot, the father of mathematical economics, enabled him to see that "business economics" (χρηματιστική of Aristotle) is that part of social science which is concerned with measurable economic phenomena of critical importance; that, without doing violence to facts, business men (οἱ χρηματιστικοί) may be assumed to seek a maximum net gain;[3] that, in a large part of business, the number of buyers and sellers is so great as to bring into evidence the play of laws of large numbers; that these laws of large numbers may be mathematically described and be made the foundation of a mathematical science of economics.

The interval between Aristotle and Cournot is a long one, but Cournot himself has taken care to put on record the connection between his thought and that of the Stagirite. The title of his first book was *Recherches sur les principes mathématiques de la théorie des richesses*, 1838; the title of his second work on economics was *Principes de la théorie des richesses*, 1863. The words in these titles common to both works describe, according to Cournot, what Aristotle meant by chrematistics. Indeed, Cournot tells us very definitely that his title is only a French translation of the word chrematistics.[4] If now we recall that by *richesse* Cournot meant anything which has a price,[5] we see how Aristotle's chrematistics has developed into the modern mathematical theory of price economics. And, curious as it may seem, Cournot made his début

---

[3] Aristotle: *Politics*, Bk. I, chap. ix. "The art of money-getting seems to be chiefly conversant about trade, and its end to be able to see where the greatest profit can be made." Bohn edition, p. 22.

[4] Cournot: *Principes de la théorie des richesses*, p. III, ". . . le mot de chrématistique, dont notre titre n'est que la traduction française. . . ."

[5] "Or, les choses auxquelles l'état des relations commerciales et les institutions civiles permettent d'attribuer une telle valeur d'échange sont celles que, dans le style moderne, on appelle des richesses." *Ibid.*, p. 2.

in the theory of riches by treating the problem of the mathematical law of demand in its relation to monopoly price, which is the very problem Thales is reputed to have meditated some two thousand years ago when he initiated astronomic and economic forecasting.

Economic Certainties

If we attempt to classify what we are in the habit of naming our thought about price phenomena, we shall find that our views may be put into three categories which we may call economic certainties, economic probabilities, and economic dreams. Into the first category we put those theorems about which we are absolutely certain; into the second, those rules that may be followed with the prospect of their being true on the average; and into the third, those products of our wishful thinking which bear so many resemblances to our dreams.

The differences in the nature of our three groups of theories will be more easily apprehended if we state at once that the criterion of "truth" varies from category to category. The criterion of truth in economic certainties is logical consistency with definitely formulated axioms, postulates, and conventions; the criterion of truth in economic probabilities is relative frequency of occurrence in empirical data; the criterion of truth in economic dreams is their conformity with our sentiments, wishes, and interests. *Veritas vos liberabit* means logical truth to the rational economist; empirical truth to the practical economist; and intuitive, wishful, or revealed truth to the utopian economist: to the synthetic economist it means empirically verified rational truth.

But, as a matter of fact, is there such a thing as an economic certainty? The reply may be given bluntly: There are undoubtedly economic certainties, and their systematic presentation constitutes rational or pure economics. Our first category, then, is made up of the theorems of rational economics. But what, precisely, is the meaning of "certain" when the word is applied to economic theorems? It means in rational economics exactly what it means in mathematics and in the rational parts of the natural sciences, namely, logical consistency with definitely formulated axioms, postulates, and conventions. The criterion of truth in rational or pure economics is logical consistency.

The certainties of the pure, or rational, economist may or may not be practically useful. Since his immediate goal is truth in the sense of logical consistency with his axioms, postulates and conventions, and since he himself determines what premises shall be his point of departure, his sheer skill in deduction and fertility in improvising hypotheses may lead him further and further afield in his theoretical Elysium. There is danger that the "certain" may be separated more and more from the "real" with the interposition of accumulating hypotheses.

This is exactly what has occurred in the development of pure, mathematical economics. The fundamental hypothesis of the science—that each factor in the economic process seeks a maximum net gain—has been distorted, technically, into "la libre concurrence absolue" (Walras): the consideration of the incessant change of all economic factors with the flow of *time* has been theoretically reserved until a first approximation shall have been made in which *time* does not figure among the variables; the world of economic realities has been replaced by the specifications of the static state. In this realm of logical certainties pure theory has been carried to a stage in which the ensemble of the interrelated factors is presented in a system of simultaneous equations.

Economic Probabilities

The way to freedom in economic theory is in our choice of a standard of truth. Implicitly, in pure theory, the criterion of truth is logical consistency with definitely formulated axioms, postulates, and conventions. Explicitly, as pure economists, we claim to have our eyes upon empirical reality alone as our guide, where, as we have seen, the criterion of truth is probable frequency of occurrence. We become aware of this conflict of standards only when we ask the question whether our rational truth squares with our empirical truth. When we definitely put this question with regard to the statical theory of general equilibrium we regretfully confess we seem to have been pursuing a mirage. There is no way of answering our question because, by the interposition of hypotheses at variance with reality, the logical construction cannot be made to square with empirical reality. The theory of general equilibrium, which rests upon the hypothesis of "la libre concurrence absolue" in a static state, cannot be made to describe the moving general equilibrium in a perpetually changing economy where absolutely free competition, in the technical sense of that term, does not and cannot exist. What shall be done in the *impasse?*

We cannot change empirical reality, but we can change *ad libitum* the axioms, postulates, and conventions that lie at the basis of our rational construction. Since, by implication, the criterion of truth in our rational construction is logical consistency with definitely formulated axioms, postulates and conventions, we do not sacrifice pure truth if we change our premises: we simply choose the form of pure truth which agrees with our empirical truth, and we wish to perfect the agreement in order that we may use our rational instruments to foreknow prospective empirical realities.

The problem, therefore, seems to be this: how shall the axioms, postulates, and conventions of pure economics be changed in order that the rational and the real may be brought into agreement? The method of the *École de Lausanne* was to start with an unreal axiom: "la libre concurrence absolue"; to postulate a static state; and to adopt a convention with regard to equilibrium, which constituted a general balance of forces in the static state, "sous un régime hypothétique de libre concurrence absolue." The synthetic economist changes the convention, the postulate, and the axiom: His conventional equilibrium is the general equilibrium which economic forces actually at work in our perpetually changing economy tend to bring about; he postulates that this equilibrium tends to occur along the lines of general trend of the varying economic factors; he abandons the axiom of "la libre concurrence absolue" in favor of the Aristotelian matter of

fact that business men go in the direction in which
"the greatest profit can be made." [6]   Starting with the
new convention, postulate, and axiom, he inquires
what the conditions are that determine the moving
equilibrium.   The investigation leads to a separation
of the rational and the empirical conditions.   The
empirical elements are the laws of demand, the laws of
supply, and the coefficients of production.   All of
these, under the new premises, are empirically determinable.   The rational elements are the new axiom,
postulate, and convention, and their logical consequences when applied deductively to the laws of
demand, the laws of supply, and the coefficients of
production.   If the premises are wisely chosen and the
empirical elements are properly evaluated, the logical
consistency of the rational construction should ensure
a final agreement with the probable frequency of the
empirical occurrences.

Economic Dreams

The economist in touch with the whole of his subject will distinguish between his ideas according as
they relate to certainties, probabilities, or dreams.   The
certainties and probabilities together are, as we have
seen, the instruments for guidance in the effort to
realize individual and group desires: they are the
means of forecasting and control.   But control with
reference to what?   How shall the desires be known

[6] The axiom is stated more accurately by Cournot: "We shall invoke
but a single axiom, or, if you prefer, make but a single hypothesis, i.e.,
that each one seeks to derive the greatest possible value from his goods
or his labour." *Researches into the Mathematical Principles of the
Theory of Wealth.* Bacon's translation, p. 44, § 20.

and, after they are known, according to what standards [7] shall they be judged good or bad?

Our economic dreams and fantasies reveal, in part, our will to believe. Throughout a long past our thought has been directed, unconsciously, toward extenuating and fortifying our dominant desires, and our economic fantasies we have called, pretentiously, economic science. Classical political economy, with great impressiveness, offered a history of the past, a science of the present, and a prophecy of the future. We recognise it now as a rationalisation of middle-class will-to-power and we understand why it waned in interest with the coming into political control of the industrial class after the passing of the Electoral Reform Bill of 1832, the repeal of the Corn Laws, and the fall of the last government of Sir Robert Peel. Marxian socialism proclaimed a philosophy of history and a "scientific socialism." It is no accident that this "scientific socialism" rests upon a theory of the exploitation of the laborer by the capitalist; for, as a whole, it is a rationalisation of lowest-class will-to-power. Such works will be produced until all men are born "free and equal." They do not yield to refutation, ridicule, or persecution. Their hold upon the popular mind is weakened only when real grievances are proved to be consequences of specified causes, and, with the mitigation of the grievances, the rationalisations disappear in desuetude.

In the seventies of the past century a new spirit

[7] "The question: what is this or that table of goods and 'morality' *worth?* must be viewed from the most widely different perspectives; especially, 'the worth for *what?*' cannot be analysed with sufficient delicacy." Nietzsche: *Genealogy of Morals.*

appeared in the treatment of economic problems. The attitude has been stigmatized as the spirit of the recluse; its product, as a philosophy of the closet. The two leading figures in the movement were Léon Walras and Stanley Jevons. Neither savant, at his entrance upon his scientific career, had lived the life of an economic anchorite, but each had earned his living in a practical occupation. Both were philosophers of scientific method; both had wide experience with many branches of science; both held as a cardinal principle that the science of economics can be developed by following the example of the natural sciences; both believed that an effective treatment of social questions can be carried forward only if practice is preceded by pure theory; both were convinced that the appropriate instrument for working out economic theory is mathematics; and both set about the elaboration of a mathematical theory of pure economics.

Pure economics is intended as a first approximation to reality. Its primary functions are to supply carefully defined concepts, to trace out the nature of interdependent causes, and to invent a technique for detecting, describing, and measuring the interplay of many causes. The first test of pure economics is its logical consistency. If this test is satisfied, it is then submitted to the ordeal of serving as a basis for a concrete description of economic actualities. The preceding chapters show how this supreme trial is made and offer reasons for supposing that it will be adequately met.

As the work of analysis and synthesis is carried out with respect to social facts of an economic order, investigation must be pushed further, by means of the same methods, to the point of taking into account those questions of morals and manners which, hitherto, have been approached chiefly with myths, dreams, and sophistries. Some two thousand years ago Cato, the Censor, posed the problem: According to Plutarch,

"A saying of Cato's was, that the Roman people fixed the value not only of such and such purple dyes, but also of such and such habits of life. 'For,' said he, 'as dyers most of all dye such colors as they see to be most agreeable, so the young men learn and zealously affect what is most popular with you.' "

Is there really a true analogy between the processes of determining the changing values of economic commodities and the fluent values of manners and morals? If there be such an analogy we are heartened for an adventure, and among the sources of our inspiration is the fact that reasoning by analogy has been the surest and most fecund method of discovery in physical science.[8] The fecundity in physics of analogical reasoning may be illustrated by the almost bodily transference of conceptions and technique developed in the theory of heat to the treatment of electricity and magnetism. The methods of Fourier, originally perfected to deal with the theory of heat, were, in the hands of Ohm and his successors, elaborately adapted to the solution of problems of electricity.

[8] An accomplished physicist, who was at the same time an historian and philosopher of scientific method, has expressed this opinion: "L'histoire de la Physique nous montre que la recherche des analogies entre deux catégories distinctes de phénomènes a peut-être été, de tous les procédés mis en oeuvre pour construire des théories physiques, la méthode la plus sûre et la plus féconde." Pierre Duhem: *La Théorie physique,* Deuxième édition, p. 140.

A particularly fruitful kind of analogical reasoning is presented when a fully developed mathematical science is brought into comparison with one less favorably circumstanced. Economics is the only social science whose quantitative phase is extensively worked out; its technique, both deductive and inductive, has assumed a mathematical form similar to that of the mathematico-physical sciences. If there be true analogies between the elementary concepts of economics and the corresponding notions in the speculations about morals and manners, there are probably similar needs as to technique, and it may be possible to develop manners and morals as sciences after the analogy of synthetic economics. Is it only a dream to expect results of value from the adventure?

Also published in

Reprints Of Economic Classics

By Henry Ludwell Moore

Economic Cycles: Their Law and Cause

By HENRY LUDWELL MOORE

Professor of Political Economy in Columbia University

8vo, $2.00

Extract from the Introduction: "There is a considerable unanimity of opinion among experts that, from the purely economic point of view, the most general and characteristic phenomenon of a changing society is the ebb and flow of economic life, the alternation of energetic, buoyant activity with a spiritless, depressed and uncertain drifting. . . . What is the cause of this alternation of periods of activity and depression? What is its law? These are the fundamental problems of economic dynamics the solution of which is offered in this Essay."

COMMENTS OF SPECIALISTS

Moore's book is so important that it is sure to be widely criticized. . . . Yet so far as the fundamental conclusions are concerned the book is so firmly grounded on a vast body of facts that its main line of argument seems unassailable. . . . Moore has gone much further than his predecessors and has removed his subject from the realm of probability to that of almost absolute certainty. Hereafter there can be little question that apart from such influences as the depreciation in gold, or great calamities like the war, the general trend of economic conditions in this country is closely dependent upon cyclical variations in the weather." — ELLSWORTH HUNTINGTON, in the *Geographical Review*.

In reply to the question: "What are the two best books you have read recently," President Butler named, as one of the two books, Professor Moore's *Economic Cycles* because of its being "an original and very stimulating study in economic theory with quick applications to practical business affairs." — NICHOLAS MURRAY BUTLER, in the *New York World*.

"Professor Moore is known among scholars as one of the keenest and most cautious of investigators. . . . His novel methods of investigation constitute an additional claim upon our interest; the problem of the crisis has never yet been approached in precisely this way." — ALVIN S. JOHNSON, in the *New Republic*.

"This book indicates a method of utilizing (economic) data . . . that is worthy of the highest commendation." — ALLEN HAZEN, in the *Engineering News*.

"If the promise of Professor Moore's convincing Essay is fulfilled, economics will become an approximately exact science. . . . If progress is made in the direction of such a goal as a result of this work, it will be the economic contribution of a century, and will usher in a new scientific epoch." — ROY G. BLAKEY, in the *Times Annalist*.

"The agricultural theory of cycles has found a new and brilliant exponent in Professor Henry L. Moore." — WESLEY CLAIR MIT-CHELL, in the *American Yearbook*.

"If his methods stand the test of experience, and can be widely adopted, the field of business may be revolutionized so far as it concerns the enterpriser because the measuring of the force of underlying, fundamental conditions will become approximately accurate and the function of the enterpriser will thereby be reduced." Magazine published by *Alexander Hamilton Institute*.

"L'auteur a mis à son service des procédés mathématiques et statistiques raffinés et élégants . . . celui-ci a écrit un livre brillant." — UMBERTO RICCI, in *Scientia*.

Laws of Wages

An Essay In Statistical Economics

By HENRY LUDWELL MOORE

Professor of Political Economy in Columbia University

8vo, $1.60

Extract from the Introduction: "In the following chapters I have endeavored to use the newer statistical methods and the more recent economic theory to extract, from data relating to wages, either new truth or else truth in such new form as will admit of its being brought into fruitful relations with the generalizations of economic science."

COMMENTS OF SPECIALISTS

"Professor Moore brings to his task a wide acquaintance with the most difficult parts of the literature of economics and statistics, a full appreciation of its large problems, a judicial spirit and a dignified style." — F. W. TAUSSIG, in the *Quarterly Journal of Economics*.

"Statistics of the ordinary official kind have often served to support the arguments of political economists. But this is the first time, we believe, that the higher statistics, which are founded on the Calculus of Probabilities, have been used on a large scale as a buttress of economic theory." — F. Y. EDGEWORTH, in the *Economic Journal*.

"Professor Moore has broken new ground in a most interesting field, and while we may differ from him in the weight to be attached to this or that result or the interpretation to be placed on some observed coefficient, we may offer cordial congratulations on the work as a whole." — G. Y. Yule, in the *Journal of the Royal Statistical Society*.

"Die Fruchtbarkeit der verwendeten Methode scheint mir durch diese Untersuchungen zweifellos erwiesen, ebenso wie die Erreichbarkeit des Ziels, die Theorie ganz dicht an die Zahlenausdrücke der wirtschaftlichen Tatsachen heranzubringen. Und das ist eine Tat, zu der der Autor nur zu beglückwünschen ist. . . . Hat das Buch auch auf der Hand liegende Fehler — in der Zukunft wird man sich seiner als der ersten klaren, einfachen und zielbewussten Darlegung und Exemplifizierung der Anwendung der 'höheren Statistik' auf ökonomische Probleme dankbar erinnern." — Joseph Schumpeter, in the *Archiv für Sozialwissenschaft und Sozialpolitik*.

"Non seulement il nous enseigne l'emploi d'une méthode qui dans de certaines limites peut être très féconde. Mais encore son habileté personnelle dans le maniement de cette méthode est très réelle. Il sait scruter les statistiques d'une façon fort pénétrante et exposer les résultats de ses recherches avec beaucoup d'élégance. Le lecteur français en particulier, appréciera l'ingéniosité avec laquelle il tire des statistiques françaises des inductions souvent nouvelles et justes." — Albert Aftalion, in the *Revue d'histoire des doctrines économiques*.

"Alcuni dei risultati ottenuti dall'autore, sono nuovi e suggestivi e da essi molte conclusioni si possono trarre (cui l'autore accenna nel capitolo finale della sua opera) sia rispetto alle teorie del salario che rispetto alla politica sociale. Il libro è insomma, ripetiamo, un contributo molto importante all'investigazione scientifica dei fenomeni economici e vorremmo che esso stimolasse parecchi altri studiosi a fare per altre industrie o per altri paesi, recerche analoghe." — Constantino Bresciani Turroni, in the *Giornale degli Economisti*.